FINE IN THE WORLD
Lumbee Language in Time and Place

Walt Wolfram

> The Language and Life Project
> NC State University

Clare Dannenberg

> University of Alaska Anchorage

Stanley Knick

> Museum of the Southeast American Indian
> UNC Pembroke
> Emeritus

Linda Oxendine

> American Indian Studies Department
> UNC Pembroke
> Emeritus

The Language and Life Project
NC State University

ISBN 978-1-4696-6140-7 (paperback)
ISBN 978-1-4696-6141-4 (ebook)

Published by The Language and Life Project
www.languageandlife.org

Distributed by UNC Press

CONTENTS

Maps & Tables

Preface

Photograph by Neal Hutcheson

Photograph by Neal Hutcheson

Few things are more symbolic of culture than language. This is no different for the Lumbee community than it is for any other community, despite the fact that the Lumbee stopped using their ancestral Native American language or languages generations ago. The story of Lumbee English is a testament to the linguistic adaptability and the resiliency of the Lumbee people, who responded to the loss of their indigenous languages by shaping the English of their European invaders into a unique emblem of Lumbee identity.

In an important sense, language reflects the status of the Lumbee people, who defy conventional stereotypes while at the same time maintain a resolute sense of who they are as an Indian people. In this book, we attempt to portray Lumbee English as it has evolved in time and place. Our hope is that readers will catch a small glimpse of the significance of language as it is interwoven into the fabric of Lumbee life. Although we have tried to avoid lapsing into excessive linguistic detail and terminology, we have probably done so with mixed success. Unfortunately, it is sometimes difficult to describe language without resorting to technical terms.

Our description has profited greatly from the support of more people than we could ever list in an acknowledgment. It starts with the late Adolph Dial, who was a source of early support and encouragement. We believe that his spirit of inquiry into history and culture lives on in this work. We are also grateful to his daughter, Mary Doris Dial-Caple, for generously allowing us access to the collection of oral history interviews conducted by her father during 1969-1971. These interviews complemented more than 150 tape-recorded interviews conducted by the staff of the North Carolina Language and Life Project from 1993 through 2000. We will never be able to thank adequately all of the people who tolerated with such grace and generosity our seemingly inane intrusions into their everyday world.

Special thanks are due to Margaret Chavis and the staff of the Indian Education Resource Center, Public Schools of Robeson County, for their valuable contributions. Former staff members Maybelle Elk, Hayes Alan Locklear, and Ed Chavis were particularly helpful in contacting members of the community, and current staff members Bruce Barton, Renee Hammonds, and Cheryl Harding were most helpful in offering photographs to complement the text. We are also indebted to photographers David Oxendine, Neal Hutcheson, and Shelley Gruendler, as well as to Amanda Robertson, who designed this book for publication. Neal Hutcheson took all of the river photos at the beginning of each chapter. Thanks to Tarra Atkinson, Karl Hunt, Stacie Jackson, Ursulla Kerns, Georgia Locklear, Ruth Locklear, Wahnema Lowery, Hubbard Lowery, Malinda Maynor, Robert Reising, Jennifer Windell, and many, many others for all of their assistance in various phases of this project.

The staff of the North Carolina Language and Life Project, in particular, Becky Childs, David Herman, Jason Miller, James Peterson, Jason Sellers, Erik R. Thomas, Ben Torbert, and Marge Wolfram, helped conduct interviews, carried out research analysis, and assisted in countless other ways. Special gratitude is due to Natalie Schilling-Estes, who planned and directed the initial phase of the linguistic survey and provided insightful linguistic analysis. Support for the project was provided by National Science

▼▼

Foundation Grant SBR-96-1633 and the William C. Friday Endowment at North Carolina State University. Jim Clark, Director of Humanities Extension/Publications at NC State and a true champion of outreach and extension programs throughout North Carolina, was instrumental in making the actual publication a reality.

A great debt, of course, is owed to the Lumbee people for their willingness to give of their language and of themselves in both obvious and less obvious ways. We would be pleased if even a little of their generous spirit and strength of character is conveyed in this work. Thanks to the Creator, for opening the doors of this project.

Walt Wolfram
North Carolina Language and Life Project
North Carolina State University

Clare Dannenberg
Virginia Polytechnical Institute and State University

Stanley Knick
Museum of the Native American Resource Center
University of North Carolina at Pembroke

Linda Oxendine
American Indian Studies Department
University of North Carolina at Pembroke

May 2002

1

LANGUAGE IN THE LUMBEE CONTEXT

The Significance of Language

Language is one of the most distinctive characteristics of the Lumbee Indians of Robeson County, North Carolina. However, contrary to popular expectations, the uniqueness of Lumbee language is not found in an ancestral Native American language. Instead, it is currently expressed in a dialect of American English. In many respects, speech is symbolic of Lumbee status as a Native American tribe—maintaining a steadfast sense of Indian identity while challenging conventional stereotypes.

Residents of Robeson County may take their words and expressions for granted, but Lumbee speech often sounds quite unusual to outsiders. As Lumbee artist Karl Hunt put it, "Anywhere away from this immediate area, they know it's different, they know it's something they've never heard before, a lot of times they're fascinated by it, because it's something different." Most Lumbee can recall occasions when curious outsiders wanted to know exactly where they came from and why they sounded so unusual—to the point of making some speakers self-conscious about the way they sound. Even within Robeson County, the Lumbee do not sound like other residents. Though they have lived side-by-side with European Americans and African Americans for several centuries now, the Lumbee have developed a unique dialect of English, which we will refer to

Photograph by Neal Hutcheson

"That's how we recognize who we are, not only by looking at someone. We know just who we are by our language. You recognize someone is from Spain because they speak Spanish, or from France because they speak French, and that's how we recognize Lumbee speakers. If we're anywhere in the country and hear ourselves speak, we know exactly who we are."

– Hayes Alan Locklear,
    Lumbee artist

"Anywhere away from the immediate area, they know it's something they've never heard before. A lot of times they're fascinated by it, because it's something that's different."

– Karl Hunt,
   Lumbee artist

(above right)
Linda Oxendine, Chair, American Indian Studies Department, University of North Carolina at Pembroke

Language in
the Lumbee Context

simply as LUMBEE ENGLISH. Not all Lumbee speak this dialect of English and many speak a mainstream variety of English, but virtually all community members are familiar with Lumbee English and readily understand it—unlike outsiders who initially may find it difficult to comprehend.

Language both sets apart and brings together. In this respect, Lumbee English is no different from any other culturally distinct variety of English. At the same time that Lumbee English separates the Lumbee from other English-speaking groups, it links together those who speak it with a common identity and heritage. Lumbee who have traveled outside the area are struck by the fact that they can usually identify another Lumbee simply by the sound of their voice. As one resident said, "It's like an immediate identification mechanism, can I talk to this person, do we share a common experience, do we have a common bond?"

What is Lumbee English? How did it develop and why is it so distinctive? What does it say about Lumbee culture and life? There are many important questions about the language of the Lumbee, ranging from those about the fate of their ancestral Native American language to those about the cultural significance of their dialect of English. In the following pages, we attempt to answer some of these questions and to explain why and how Lumbee English has evolved.

The story of Lumbee language should not be reduced to speculation about what happened to the Native American languages that were once spoken by their ancestors. Instead, it is about the linguistic creativity, flexibility, and resiliency of a cultural group that has shaped and reshaped its identity through available language resources, in this case, mainly from English. Though the Lumbee today speak only English, their dialect of English has become a natural part of who they are and how they define themselves. Even the Congressional Act of 1956 recognizes this fact when it states:

> Whereas by reason of tribal legend, coupled with distinctive appearance and *manner of speech*…shall, after the ratification of this Act, be known and designated as the Lumbee Indians of North Carolina.

The loss of the ancestral language or languages by the Lumbee is a cultural, historical, and scientific tragedy, but the irrepressible and malleable nature of their culture in maintaining language identity through the replacement language, English, is a testament to the adaptability of human nature and the strength of the connection between language and culture.

Pow-wows, homecoming, and other cultural celebrations are an important part of community life for many Lumbee.

(above right)
Tobacco farms have been a part of Lumbee agriculture for centuries.

The Lumbee Community

No one living in the southeastern sandhills of North Carolina needs to be told who the Lumbee are. Nor do the Lumbee themselves. As one Lumbee told an inquiring reporter seeking to determine the exact Native American roots of the Lumbee, "We know who we are, we know, we have always known; y'all are the ones who are trying to identify something." Though outsiders have been debating their precise cultural status and historical origin for well over a century now, the question of who the Lumbee are is largely a matter of external speculation rather than internal confusion. Barbara Braveboy-Locklear (Knick 2000:77) summarizes it succinctly:

> Who are the Lumbee? Our identity is rooted in our Native American culture. Our struggle to prove our identity is caught between continuous theoretical debates on our origin. Yet we know who we are and recognize our own. For centuries, in Native tradition, we have passed on to our relations generation after generation the philosophy and practice of reverence and respect for the interwoven fabric of existence.

The name *Lumbee* has been known for centuries (Knick 2000; Rudes 2001), although they were previously assigned the names

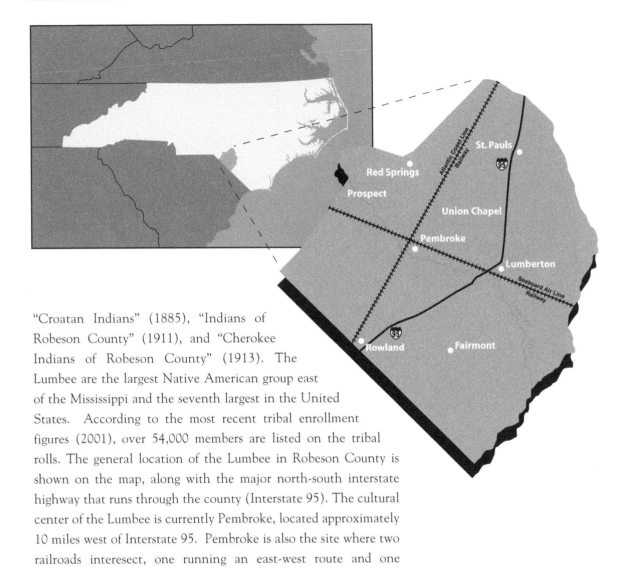

"Croatan Indians" (1885), "Indians of Robeson County" (1911), and "Cherokee Indians of Robeson County" (1913). The Lumbee are the largest Native American group east of the Mississippi and the seventh largest in the United States. According to the most recent tribal enrollment figures (2001), over 54,000 members are listed on the tribal rolls. The general location of the Lumbee in Robeson County is shown on the map, along with the major north-south interstate highway that runs through the county (Interstate 95). The cultural center of the Lumbee is currently Pembroke, located approximately 10 miles west of Interstate 95. Pembroke is also the site where two railroads interesect, one running an east-west route and one running a north-south route. The location of Pembroke and several other settlements such as Prospect and Union Chapel are shown in the inset of Robeson County.

Although the Lumbee live in surrounding counties and in cities such as Greensboro and Raleigh, as well as in other states, Robeson County has the largest population of Lumbee and is the homeland of the Lumbee, with almost 47,000 Native Americans counted in the 2000 US Census.

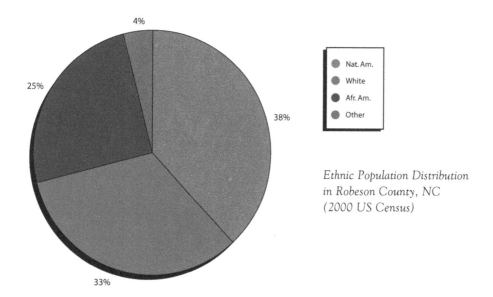

Legend:
- Nat. Am.
- White
- Afr. Am.
- Other

Ethnic Population Distribution in Robeson County, NC (2000 US Census)

Only one other county east of the Mississippi River has a plurality of Native Americans.

Robeson County is also home to large populations of European Americans and African Americans, as well as a small but rapidly growing population of Hispanics. The most recent census shows that the Lumbee population in Robeson County has grown more than any other group in the county in the last decade, both in terms of actual population and in proportion to other ethnic groups. The proportions of the major ethnic groups in Robeson County are illustrated in the population chart.

To give a perspective on the significance of the population figures for Robeson County, consider several facts. Robeson County has more than eight times as many Native Americans as any other non-metropolitan county east of the Mississippi River; in fact, no other non-metropolitan county has more than 6,000 Native Americans. Furthermore, only one other county east of the Mississippi River (Menominee County, Wisconsin) has a plurality of Native Americans. In contrast, counties such as Graham and Cherokee in Western North Carolina, primary locations for the Eastern Band of Cherokee, are made up of less than 10 percent Native Americans.

The concentrated population of Lumbee in southeastern North Carolina has important implications for language differ-

The early days of "Croatan Normal School," established for training Lumbee teachers.

ences. Isolated ethnic concentrations offer an ideal context for maintaining language distinctiveness. The town of Pembroke (population approximately 2,400) is well over 80 percent Lumbee and the community of Prospect (population approximately 700) is over 95 percent Lumbee, making the Lumbee presence dominant in these locales and Lumbee English a practical, everyday norm for communication.

The Lumbee not only were the first Native American group in North Carolina to petition the state government and to win formal recognition and entitlements in the 1880s, but they were also the first to receive funds from the state government to create an Indian normal school in 1887, now known as the University of North Carolina at Pembroke. Federally, the Lumbee have limited recognition with no funding appropriation from the Bureau of Indian Affairs, and they are not currently eligible for reservation land.

The Lumbee are now gaining visibility, but they are still surprisingly unknown outside of southeastern North Carolina. In part, this is because of their ambiguous, qualified status with the federal government. They have also been subjected to several name changes, which may have led to questions about their

Indian State Normal College has now become the University of North Carolina at Pembroke.

permanence and cultural "purity"—despite the fact that there is ample archaeological evidence that Native Americans have inhabited the Robeson County region continuously for up to 14,000 years (Knick 1988, 1993).

The current status of the Lumbee may be the result of the permeable and changing ethnic boundaries among different Native American tribal groups in the region that is the homeland of the Lumbee. In fact, historical and archaeological evidence (Knick 2000) and linguistic evidence (Rudes 2001) of different cultures in this region in both prehistoric and historic times suggest that the Lumbee of today developed from a conglomerate of different tribes in the region.

In part, the current, ambiguous status of the Lumbee may also be the unfortunate result of their early adoption of English. The stereotypical notion of Indians is that they should speak a Native American language and be strictly bounded culturally. This mold does not fit the Lumbee. The Lumbee learned English relatively early in their contact with Europeans, giving up their ancestral language or languages considerably earlier than some other Native American groups. For example, Native American groups in the western United States first encountered English speakers a couple of centuries after those inhabiting Coastal Carolina; as a result, some of them lost their indigenous language much later than the Lumbee.

LANGUAGE IN
THE LUMBEE CONTEXT

8

Photograph by Neal Hutcheson

"These Indians (had) roads connecting the distinct settlements with their principal seat on the Lumbee, as The Lumber River was then called."

– Hamilton McMillan, 1888

Although the cultural development of the Lumbee does not fit the European stereotype of a static, homogeneous Indian tribe, it hardly threatens their sense of cultural identity. All cultures, including Native American, British, and American cultures, constantly change and reconfigure themselves through various unions that do not threaten their ultimate sense of cultural identity. In fact, such evolution, including the remolding of language, may actually strengthen the base of cultural integrity, and the conglomerate culture may have a stronger sense of cultural identity than the cultures that contributed to it.

The Word *Lumbee*

Perhaps no term is more indicative of the Lumbee situation than the term *Lumbee* itself. Many outsiders assume that this term is simply an invented word made up in the 1950s, but this is highly questionable. The term *Lumbee* was attested well over a century ago (Knick 2000:66), and the Lumber River was formerly referred to as the Lumbee River. The state legislator and historian, Hamilton McMillan, wrote in 1888: "These Indians [had] roads connecting the distinct settlements with their principal seat on the Lumbee, as the Lumber River was then called" (quoted in Knick 2000:66). Given the Native American tradition of sharing the names of rivers and groups—for example, Santee, Wateree,

Photograph by Neal Hutcheson

"Bring me a cup of that ellick in here, I want some ellick."

– Georgia Locklear

Congaree, Pee Dee, and so forth—it seems likely that the term Lumbee may, in fact, be a long-term reference to those who lived by the Lumbee River.

It may be mere coincidence, but it should also be noted that many names for Native American groups in the region end in a final –ee, though this spelling may actually be pronounced in several different ways. After examining the possibility that the term Lumbee may have come from a Native American language, Catawban-Siouan language specialist Blair Rudes (forthcoming) speculates that Lumbee derives from a coastal dialect form of Catawban meaning "bank of a river" (*yą́ʔbe* or *rą́ʔbe* in Piedmont Catawban), pronounced something like *yahmp-bee* though it is impossible to give equivalent sounds in English.[1] Related terms for this group of Native Americans found in earlier citations include the labels *Aranbe*, *Ilapi*, and *Herape*. According to Rudes, this name was assigned during the time of the expansive, multilingual Cofitachique chiefdom that stretched from the Atlantic seaboard to the Appalachian Mountains when de Soto first reached the Piedmont area of the Carolinas in 1541 (Rudes forthcoming). Whatever the origin of the term Lumbee, it cannot simply be concluded that it is a recent innovation that is related to the English word *lumber*.

It is just as easy, and perhaps more realistic, to speculate that European Americans took the Native American name for a river and people, *Lumbee*, and assumed that it was related to the term *lumber* in a process known as FOLK ETYMOLOGY. In this process, a word is reinterpreted so that it makes sense in terms of existing words. For example, reinterpreting *Alzheimers Disease* as *Old Timer's Disease* or *garter snake* as *garden snake* are folk etymologies because the words are modified to fit existing phrases that make common sense. In Charlotte, North Carolina, the name of a well-

---

[1] The vowel *a*, for example, is nasalized like some of the vowels of French, and the symbol [ʔ] represents a glottal stop as in the pronunciation of the *t* in *bottle* or *button* in some dialects of English. The y sound is pronounced something like the *ll* of Spanish words like *llamar* or *calle*, which is related to the *l* sound.

known creek, *Sugar Creek*, came from a Sugaree Indian word *sugaw* (meaning 'group of huts') precisely through this type of folk etymology. That is, English speakers heard the Native American term *sugaw* and simply assumed it was related to a similar sounding English word *sugar*. It is not far-fetched to suggest that European Americans may have taken the indigenous term *Lumbee* and modified it into a word that made sense to them—*lumber*. The modification of the term Lumbee into Lumber certainly would make sense in terms of the county's largest city, Lumberton, so named because of its role in the early lumber industry. Whatever its historical roots might be, it is clear that the term Lumbee is not a recent innovation and that it has come to be associated exclusively with a Native American community strongly connected to the river.

Lumbee English

Lumbee English is distinguished by several different aspects of language: vocabulary, or lexicon; pronunciation; and sentence structure, or grammar. In defining the dialect, however, it is important to understand that it is differentiated primarily by the combinations of structures rather than by the existence of exclusively Lumbee expressions. The delimitation of Lumbee English does not rest or fall on the identification of features that are used only by members of the Lumbee community even though there are some unique items. A few distinctive words, such as *ellick* (coffee with sugar), *yerker* (mischievous child), and *on the swamp* (neighborhood) are mostly restricted to the Lumbee, but words like *fatback* (fat meat of a hog), *mommuck* (mess up), and *head'nes'* (overwhelming, very bad) are shared with other dialects in the Southern Coastal Plain and beyond. We will say more about some of the words, as well as other features of the dialect, in our comparison of Lumbee English with other dialects.

Pronunciation features of Lumbee English combine patterns from the Outer Banks coastal region and features often associated with Appalachian English as spoken in the highlands to the west

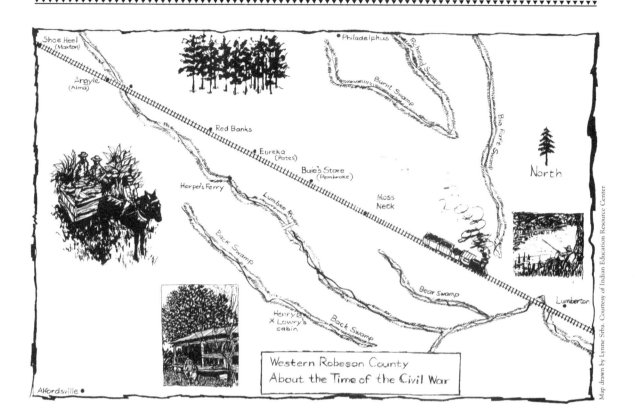

Map drawn by Lynne Srba. Courtesy of Indian Education Resource Center

of Robeson County. For example, older Lumbee residents in isolated communities such as Prospect sometimes pronounce *side* and *time* something like *soid* and *toim*, more like the traditional pronunciation of these vowels on the Outer Banks of North Carolina than the widespread unglided Southern pronunciation of *tahd* and *tahm*. *Tobacco* and *potato* may be pronounced as *'baccer* and *'tater*, combining the loss of an unstressed syllable and an intrusive *r* in the final syllable in a way that parallels both the coastal dialect of North Carolina and Smoky Mountain speech. When combined with pronunciations such as *tar* for *tire* and *far* for *fire*, the accent strikes listeners as a slightly modified version of Appalachian speech.

Several prominent grammatical features also characterize Lumbee English. One of the dialect icons of Lumbee English is the use of *bes* in sentences such as *That's how it bes* or *The dogs bes doing that*. Another feature is the use of *weren't* with past tense *be* in sentences such as *It weren't me* or *I weren't down there*, a pattern shared with coastal dialects in the Mid-Atlantic South. Also, Lumbee English uses a form of *be* where other dialects use *have*, as in *I'm been there already* for *I've been there already* or *He be took the food* for *He has taken the food*.

As we noted, it is possible to point to a few specific words, pronunciations, and sentences associated with Lumbee English, but its definition is found in the combination of structures brought together in the dialect mix rather than unique dialect features *per se*. In this respect, Lumbee English is no different from any other regional, social, or ethnic dialect of English. What is most significant is the fact that no other dialect of English has blended its linguistic ingredients in exactly the same way.

Although we have discussed Lumbee English as if it were a single, unified dialect of English, this is also a stereotype. In fact, there are a lot of differences in the speech of Lumbees within Robeson County. First, there is variation in the extent to which different speakers, or groups of speakers, use the dialect forms commonly associated with what we call Lumbee English. Some speakers use a majority of the features described for the VERNAC-ULAR version of the dialect, that is, the version most different from so-called Standard English; other speakers use very few of these features. Linguists are prone to describe dialects in their ideal, most vernacular form, but the reality is that Lumbee English, like any other vernacular dialect, exists on a scale in which different speakers may use more or less of these features. Whether or not individual speakers use the vernacular variety, it is safe to say that virtually all Lumbee readily understand it.

Speakers with more extended contact and professional training are less likely to use the full range of vernacular structures while older speakers living in isolated communities are more likely to use these features. But it is again not quite that simple. Speakers often feel the need to balance local speech identity with their presentation to an outside world that has little knowledge of or appreciation for Lumbee English. Many speakers can therefore shift their speech, depending on whom they are talking to, what they are talking about, and where the conversation is taking place.

There are also some generational differences in Lumbee English. Like any other variety of language, Lumbee English is not static; it is always changing in one way or another. Thus, older speakers may use some forms that younger speakers do not and vice versa. In examining Lumbee English for speakers who represent well over a century in time, we have found some significant changes in the dialect as patterns of contact with the outside world, interaction within the community itself, and cultural lifestyles have shifted. For example, older speakers in more isolated communities such as Prospect are more likely to say *soid* for *side* or *toime* for *time*, to use the prefix *a-* before verbs as in *She was a-fishin'*, and to preserve some of the older vocabulary items (*toten*, *frock*) that have faded from the active speech of younger Lumbee residents. But this does not mean that the dialect is becoming extinct. Some features are maintaining themselves and even getting stronger. For example, the use of *weren't* in sentences like *I weren't there* or *She weren't here* is stronger among younger speakers, and the use of *I'm* for *I've* in sentences like *I'm been there* (*I've been there*) persists in the speech of younger vernacular speakers. So although there are particular dialect features associated with different generations of speakers, the dialect is quite resilient. Despite the fact that Lumbee English today is not exactly the same as it was a couple of generations ago, it remains quite distinct and robust among younger speakers.

Finally, there are some apparent regional differences in Lumbee English. Robeson County encompasses 948 square miles, and there are a number of different Lumbee communities situated throughout the region. Furthermore, there was not always regular contact between different communities. Pembroke is considered to be the current center of the Lumbee community, while Prospect is considered to be the oldest and most important Lumbee cultural community in terms of tradition. Depending on how finely one draws dividing lines, there are anywhere from 2 to 20 other

Lumbee sub-communities, many of which take their names from the large swamps that dominate the local landscape: Back Swamp, Burnt Swamp, Bear Swamp, and so forth (Dial 1969-1971; Schilling-Estes 2000).

In a comparison of different generations of speech in the communities of Prospect and Union Chapel, Schilling-Estes (2000) found that the use of the *toim* for *time* pronunciation was clearly favored for older speakers from Prospect and, to a lesser degree, by Union Chapel (See also Brewer and Reising 1982). Kerns' (2001) study of different vocabulary words in the communities of Prospect and Pembroke did not, however, show a community-based difference for vocabulary that was as clear as the differences for the pronunciation of the vowel in *time* and *side*. Sub-regional differences among Lumbee communities within Robeson County must thus be factored into the reality of language variation though they are probably fading among the younger generations.

Depending on how finely one draws dividing lines, there are anywhere from 2 to 20 other Lumbee sub-communities, many of which take their names from the large swamps that dominate the local landscape: Back Swamp, Burnt Swamp, Bear Swamp, and so forth (Dial 1969-1971; Schilling-Estes 2000)

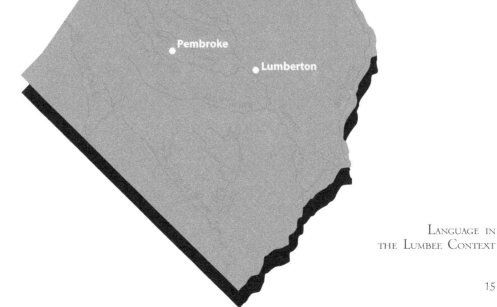

Listener Group	Lumbee	White	African American
	Correct Ethnic Identification		
Total Listeners (N = 45)	83%	70%	91%
Younger Lumbee (N = 25) (Under 16 Years)	77%	70%	88%
Older Lumbee (N = 20) (Over 21 Years)	90%	70%	95%

Despite some of the differences among speakers from different backgrounds, from different communities, and from different generations, it seems clear that Lumbee English is still recognizable as a distinct dialect—at least to those in the immediate area. To examine the extent to which Lumbee speakers are identifiable to listeners, Wolfram (2000) and Hammonds (2000) designed a simple speaker identification task. Twelve anonymous passages of 20-30 seconds each were taken from natural conversational interviews conducted by the staff of the North Carolina Language and Life project, four from each of the three major Robeson County ethnic groups. The vernacular dialect samples, which were neutral with respect to ethnically identifiable content, included two men and two women from each ethnic group, one younger and one older speaker. The listening task was then administered to several different groups of speakers, including younger and older Lumbee residents in Robeson County (Hammonds 2000). Listeners were simply asked to identify the speakers on the tape as White, Lumbee, or African American. The results of the identification task for the older and younger Lumbee from Robeson County are given on the chart.

The results from the listening task show that the Lumbee can indeed recognize the ethnic identity of Robeson County speakers based simply on a speech sample. In fact, the overall correct identification for the Lumbee speakers, over 80 percent, was higher than it was for White speakers. Our empirical research clearly supports the claim that Lumbee English is recognizable as an ethnic dialect by the Lumbee; the dialect is neither White nor African American speech, but distinctly Lumbee.

Lumbee English and Language Correctness

The vernacular version of Lumbee English is not the English used by the media, the government, or the educational system. Verb uses such as *be* in *It bes that way, I'm been there* and subject-verb agreement patterns like *People goes there* are hardly considered to be socially sanctioned mainstream, or "Standard English", and there is little likelihood that they will be deemed standard norms in the immediate future. The nonstandard status of some features associated with Lumbee English has sometimes led educators and others to the conclusion that Lumbee English is nothing more than "bad" or "corrupt" English—an unworthy approximation of Standard English. Even some Lumbee educators and professionals make this assessment. However, the relationship of Lumbee English to mainstream, standard varieties of English is much more complex than its categorical rejection as "bad English."

Most people recognize that there is a relationship between power and language, but they don't realize how arbitrarily language fits into this equation. If a socially dominant group used structures like *People goes there* or *I'm been there*, these structures would be considered perfectly proper and standard—and any other way of using these verbs would be considered incorrect or nonstandard. As a matter of fact, at one point in the history of English, these structures were considered to be quite correct uses of English, along with the use of the prefix *a-* (pronounced something like *uh*) in sentences like *They were a-huntin'*, the double negative of sentences like *They didn't go nowhere*, and many more structures now associated with nonstandard speech. It may seem surprising, but most of the structures associated with Lumbee English were, at one point in the history of English, considered to be perfectly proper and acceptable, and any other way of speaking would have been considered incorrect or nonstandard.

Photograph by David Oxendine

Linda Oxendine teaches Lumbee history, including the role of language in the past and present.

*Purnell Swett High School students,
Nicole Jacobs, Lakeshia Jacobs, Beth
Lowery and Courtney Neville*

So what happened? It is not difficult to figure out what has happened if we look at the social relations among different groups in society. Over time, as the English language changed, structures retained by non-mainstream, socially subordinate groups became socially stigmatized, following on the heels of the cultural derogation of these groups. Patterns of cultural subjugation routinely lead to linguistic subordination as well (Lippi-Green 1997). Language and dialect differences that involve groups unequal in their power relations are subjected to the LINGUISTIC INFERIORITY PRINCIPLE (Wolfram and Schilling-Estes 1998:6), in which the language variety of a socially subordinate group is judged as linguistically unworthy by comparison with the language of the socially dominant group. This is true for any culturally subordinate group, so that the speech of the Lumbee, African Americans, Hispanics, poor White Appalachians, and other socially subordinate groups is routinely rejected by the dominant culture—those with political, educational, and economic clout.

What is important to note in this equation, however, is that the sociopolitical evaluation has nothing to do with the linguistic integrity of the particular language structures. Linguists, who study the intricate patterning of language apart from its social evaluation, stand united against the definition of any dialect as a corrupt version of the socially favored variety. As stated in a resolution unanimously adopted by the Linguistic Society of America (1997), "all human language systems—spoken, signed, and written—are fundamentally regular" and characterizations of socially disfavored varieties as "slang, mutant, defective, ungrammatical, or broken English are incorrect and demeaning." One of the great joys in studying Lumbee English, or any other vernacular variety of English for that matter, is discovering the intricate, systematic patterning of various dialect forms. Linguistic researchers have provided extensive, detailed analyses focused on particular structures of Lumbee English, including the use of *I'm* in *I'm been there* (Wolfram 1996; Dannenberg forthcoming), the use of *bes* in *That's how it bes* (Dannenberg and Wolfram 1998), the absence of *be* in *They nice* (Dannenberg 2000), the use of *weren't* in *I weren't there* (Wolfram and Sellers 1999), and the pronunciation of the vowel in *time* and *side* (Brewer and Reising 1982; Schilling-Estes 2000). In each case, the analysis reveals precise, systematic patterning that demonstrates structural linguistic integrity and historical continuity.

It is sometimes assumed that the description of vernacular patterns is a thinly disguised attempt to undermine the sovereignty of the kinds of English deemed appropriate in government, education, and the media, but this is not the case. The structural study of the features of Lumbee English is not intended to challenge the usefulness of mainstream, standard varieties of English. The use of Standard English in educational and government institutions—and in the writing of this book—is fully acknowledged and respected. Furthermore, expectations for Lumbee who operate within the broader society are no different from those for speakers of other dialects of English.

There are, however, a couple of points that must be kept in mind as we recognize the role and the power of standard English in American society. First, it must be remembered that language differences are not a matter of good and bad language per se, but a matter of power relations between groups. If the Lumbee were the dominant social group in the United States, then Lumbee English would be the standard dialect and all others would be considered inferior and "corrupt" versions of English. That assessment may seem strange, but it is, in fact, a true reflection of the sociopolitical reality of language differences.

Second, it must be recognized that there is sometimes competition between the functions of standard English and the local dialect that reflects the tender balance of people caught between different worlds. In the home community, people are expected to stay in touch with their local cultural and linguistic roots, whereas the wider society expects people to conform to a different set of norms. There is a natural tension between the role of language as it represents local identity and heritage on the one hand, and relationships of power in society on the other. For as long as there has been formal education for the Lumbee—regularly since the 1880s—there have been attempts to eradicate Lumbee English and these attempts have not yet succeeded. So why haven't these attempts been successful? Perhaps a more appropriate question is why language differences persist among the Lumbee in the face of constant pressure to assimilate to the norms of standard English. At its core, there is a struggle between the pressure to maintain local cultural identity and distinctiveness in language and the pressure to assimilate to external norms—in language and in other behaviors. That the Lumbee community has managed to maintain this linguistic balance for so long without assimilating completely is a testament to the strength of their linguistic identity and solidarity and to the power of their culture.

Unfortunately, language in the Lumbee community has been subjected to a type of double jeopardy. The Lumbee initially adapted their language to the sociopolitical and economic demands of European encroachment. In the long run, this accommodation has been used as a reason for denying them full recognition as a Native American tribe, since an ancestral tribal language certainly would have been one of the clearest indicators of cultural distinctiveness and continuous presence. But the Lumbee creative linguistic response, which molded the language of their intruders into a distinct ethnic dialect, is now dismissed by some as nothing more than "bad English" with no linguistic integrity.

Lumbee English is certainly different from standard English and is not the language of mainstream America, but it has linguistic authenticity and serves an essential, symbolic role in marking cultural and ethnic identity. There can be no other reason for its survival in the face of persistent pressure to assimilate to the language of mainstream America.

2

THE ANCESTRAL LANGUAGE TRADITION

The historical circumstances involving the Lumbee make it difficult to trace the roots of Lumbee language. To begin with, there
is little early historical documentation of the languages of the
Lumbee River region. Although some Native American languages
along the Carolina coast and Piedmont were documented as early
as the sixteenth century, the region by the Lumbee River was not
included in this survey. A second difficulty in documentation
relates to the relatively early acquisition of the English language
by the Lumbee. By the mid-1700s, the Lumbee were reportedly no
longer reliant exclusively on their ancestral language for communication, at least in their interactions with outsiders (Dial and
Eliades 1975). While the early use of English may have been
helpful for maintaining interaction with English-speaking groups,
it obscured ancestral language roots.

A third difficulty in speculating about the ancestral language
roots of the Lumbee comes from the cultural dynamics of the area.
Archaeological evidence (Mathis and Garner 1986; Knick 1988,
1993) and linguistic evidence (Rudes forthcoming) suggest that
the region by the Lumbee River was a zone of cultural interaction
for thousands of years before the arrival of Europeans, extending
into the colonial period. It is, in fact, quite possible that the
Lumbee community developed not from a single, homogeneous
cultural group but from a conglomerate of Native Americans
(Knick 2000). While such a model does not match the American

*As early as the 1730s Europeans
moving through Southeast North
Carolina reported that they encountered "a large group of Indians,
speaking English, tilling the soil, own-
ing slaves, and practicing the arts of
civilized life." (McMillan, 1888)*

stereotype of Native American tribal purity, the reality of cultural dynamics suggests that there were indeed many cases of cultural convergence as well as independence among Native Americans— for reasons that range from trade and economic interdependence to wars and disease.

The prehistoric movements of Native American groups in the area, the shifting dynamics of Native American language groups, and the relatively early replacement of Native American languages with English make it extremely difficult, if not impossible, to identify a single ancestral language lineage for the Lumbee. Despite these complexities, an examination of the historic Native American language situation reveals some clues about the nature and status of the ancestral Native American language(s) that might have been involved in the emergence of Lumbee English.

Native American Languages in the Carolinas

At least three prominent language families existed in the Carolinas at the dawn of the North American historic period— Eastern Siouan, Iroquoian, and Algonquian—and each of these families was represented by a number of different languages. Linguists use the term LANGUAGE FAMILY to refer to the fact that different languages are related because they developed historically from the same language. Within language families, however, there may be many different mutually unintelligible, individual languages. For example, German and English are part of the same language family historically, but there is virtually no intelligibility between them today. The reconstruction of language family relationships is based on the detailed, formal comparison of the sound, word, and sentence correspondences among languages that indicate related items, or COGNATES. For example, there are a number of similarities in English and German that demonstrate their historical relationship; English-German word pairs such as *apple* and *apfel*, *mother* and *mutter*, and *hand* and

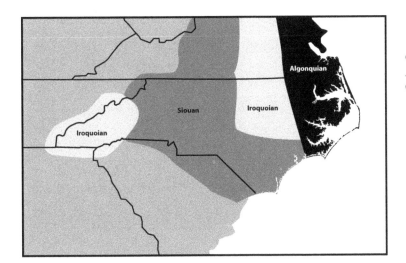

Geographical distribution of Native American language families in North Carolina prior to European exploration

hande are obviously cognates even though German and English are no longer mutually intelligible.

The observation that there were several major Native American language families in the Carolinas historically is merely the tip of the language iceberg. Based on earlier documentation, it is reasonable to conclude that there were dozens of different Native American languages spoken at one time in the Carolinas (Goddard 1996). The Eastern Siouan language family constituted the largest group of languages in North Carolina, spanning across the Piedmont east into the inner Coastal Plain and across both the Virginia and South Carolina borders, as illustrated in the above map. The application of linguistic procedures for reconstructing time depth in historical language relations (Goddard 1996) suggests that the Eastern branch of Siouan languages was probably the earliest and most expansive language family in the Carolinas, having been there for thousands of years. The primary language spoken in the Carolinas was probably Catawba (technically part of the Siouan-Catawban family according to Rudes, forthcoming) but Cheraw (Sera) and Jacamar were spoken close to the site of Robeson County today, and Tutelo, Occaneeechi, and Saponi were spoken to the north closer to and extending into present-day Virginia. Of the Eastern Siouan languages in North Carolina, none is spoken today, although efforts have begun to reintroduce Tupelo words among the Haliwa-Saponi. Collected word lists, grammatical and phonological sketches, and some texts from these languages are the only records of their existence (Gatschet 1900a; Siebert 1945; Swanton 1936).

Algonquian languages in North Carolina included Roanoac (Roanoke), Hatteras, and Pomouic (Pamlico), among others. These languages were spoken in the Outer Coastal Plain and the Outer Banks, stretching northward into Virginia. Although there are questions about the Algonquian migration into the Carolinas from the north (cf. Fiedel 1991; Luckenbach, Clark, and Levy 1987), it is estimated that Algonquian speakers were settled in the North Carolina region for at least a thousand years before the European incursion (Wetmore 1975).

Thomas Hariot, a member of Sir Walter Raleigh's first British settlement in coastal Carolina in 1585, documented Carolina Algonquian in the late 16th century. Hariot mainly recorded lexical items such as place, personal, and animal names, but many of his records, which also may have included a dictionary, have been lost. The only other surviving and reliable documentation of Carolina Algonquian was made in the early 1700s by John Lawson, the general surveyor in North Carolina who collected a word list of Pamlico. The Carolina Algonquian languages, like the Siouan languages, are now almost if not completely extinct.

Iroquoian languages in North Carolina included Tuscarora, Nottoway, Meherrin, and Cherokee. The first three languages were spoken in the eastern part of North Carolina on the Piedmont rim and part of the inner Coastal Plain, and Cherokee was spoken in the western portion of the state within the Appalachian Mountains. Although the Cherokee and Tuscarora languages were spoken a couple of hundred miles apart from each other, they are very distant linguistic relatives. Cherokee represents the Southern Iroquoian language branch while the others are more related to the Northern Iroquoian branch, including such languages as Mohawk and Oneida. Both Cherokee and Tuscarora are still spoken. Tuscarora is used by the Tuscarora tribe in the Northeast United States, descendants of the North Carolina Tuscaroran group that moved northward in the 18th century. There are only vestiges of Tuscarora found in North Carolina today, but some Robeson County Native Americans today assert Tuscaroran heritage. Cherokee, on the other hand, is still spoken in the Appalachian Mountain region, the tribe's historical homeland, and in Oklahoma where the majority of the Cherokee Nation was forced to move in the early 19th century during the infamous Trail of Tears march.

Native American languages in North Carolina did not exist in isolation from one another or even from languages in other regions prior to European exploration. Interaction between Native American language groups existed in a variety of forms, including trade, warfare, and shared cultural practices. Language adaptation as a result of this contact would have been greatest among the groups at the borders of linguistic regions or for those groups located along established trade routes. Native American multilingualism and a type of Native American LINGUA FRANCA, or language used for wider communication, may have been adopted by groups of Native Americans who had more regular contact with one another in the Southeast before European contact (Silverstein 1996).

As Europeans began infiltrating the North Carolina area, the language situation for the Native Americans became much more unstable, and in many ways, more dire. European attitudes about the Native American populations in the Southeast ranged from fascination to fear, but rarely did the attitudes include a genuine inclination towards equality and tolerance for indigenous cultural practice. In fact, most European contact was forceful, resulting in severe shifts of power to Europeans. These relations fueled the formation of pidgin varieties of English in the Southeastern coastal regions. A PIDGIN LANGUAGE is a modified hybrid language based on the vocabulary of the socially dominant language group; it develops through the attempts of speakers to communicate when

THE ANCESTRAL
LANGUAGE TRADITION

27

One popular belief about the Lumbee connects them to the Lost Colony.

they do not have a common language. In the history of North America, there have been a number of American Indian Pidgin languages, including one that may have existed in parts of the Southeast (Silverstein 1996). In most instances, however, English simply overwhelmed Native American languages. In some instances this shift took place within a couple of generations, but in other cases the shift to English was more gradual, and bilingualism lasted a number of generations before English replaced the heritage language.

Though there is no indisputable evidence to suggest exactly when or where the present-day Lumbee community was formed and precisely what language or languages they spoke before the European incursion, there are two hypotheses. One hypothesis is that the present-day Lumbee Indians were originally situated on the coast and then migrated to the area now known as Robeson County. In brief, this hypothesis suggests that the group of Roanoke colonists who disappeared during the two years when John White traveled back to England blended their culture with that of the Hatteras Indians, who then migrated south and inland toward the Lumbee River. Lumbee leader and historian Adolph Dial argues:

> While proof of Lumbee descent from the Lost Colony, in the form of birth records and other documents is most unlikely to be found, the circumstantial evidence, when joined with logic, unquestionably supports the Lumbee tradition that there was a real and lasting connection with the Raleigh Settlement. The survival of colonists' names, the uniqueness of the Lumbee dialect in the past, the oral traditions, the demography of sixteenth century North Carolina, the mobility of the Indian people, human adaptability and the isolation of Robeson County, all prove the "Lost Colony" theory. (Dial and Eliades 1975: 13)

If the Lumbee migrated from the coast, they would probably have spoken an Algonquian language when they arrived along the Lumbee River. And if they did, they were certainly not the first Native American group to arrive there; other Native Americans were there long before that period, so that a coastal group might have blended with them.

  The other hypothesis argues that the Lumbee and their ancestors inhabited the Robeson County area continuously for a much longer period. As noted, archaeological, anthropological, and linguistic evidence suggest continuous Native American occupation of the Robeson County area since prehistory (Knick 1988, 1993; Rudes forthcoming). This does not, however, mean that there was a single, homogenous group of Native Americans there throughout the prehistory and history of the region. In fact, the archaeological evidence suggests that Native American cultural differences developed in the area at different times. So it is still quite possible that the Lumbee developed from a blending of Native American cultures existing in the region and that more than one language was spoken in the area at an earlier period. The Lumbee River was apparently along a trade route and different Native American influences affected the area over time, so it

Indian historians Adolph Dial (top) and Lew Barton offered views on the origin of the Lumbee community.

THE ANCESTRAL
LANGUAGE TRADITION

29

would have been very natural for an amalgamated community to emerge. (Knick 2000).

The two hypotheses are not necessarily exclusive, since it is possible that a migrating group from the Outer Banks speaking an Algonquian language encountered an Eastern Siouan tribe residing in Robeson County at the time. At the same time, the Lumbee River was not too far removed from the Iroquoian language, Tuscarora, to the north. Even if the Lumbee did not migrate inland from the coastal region, contact with Iroquoian and Algonquian languages was likely. The location of the Lumbee and the navigational routes available through the Lumbee River and the Cape Fear River to the north permitted direct travel to the coast. It is therefore reasonable to speculate that the ancestors of the Lumbee might well have been familiar with languages representing all three major language families of the Carolinas, and that the Lumbee emerged as a conglomerate group from a multilingual ancestral language situation.

It is important to understand that speculation about the development of Lumbee culture from a multilingual conglomerate does not diminish their cultural validity in the least. Cultural groups existing in multilingual language situations are no less real than those that come from monolingual ancestral communities. There are, in fact, many situations in European language history where a distinctive language entity developed through extensive mixing of quite different languages, including the development of English in the British Isles, but this does not invalidate the cultural group that developed out of this situation. Nor does it invalidate the language; if it did, then it would nullify the English language, which went through several periods of extensive mixing with other languages. The same standard should be applied to the Lumbee. Certainly, the longstanding existence of Native Americans along the Lumbee River in the region now identified as Robeson County and the persistence of the current-day Lumbee community are sufficient testament to their cultural and linguistic integrity.

Given the evolving power relations between Native American peoples in North Carolina and the presumed transitional zone of Native American languages in the region at the time, it would certainly not be surprising for a rapid transition from Native American languages to English to take place among the Lumbee. The rapid decline of Native American languages in the United States is a well-attested cultural crisis (Hinton 1994). Within the last century more than 25 Native American languages—not dialects but separate languages—have been lost in California alone. So the loss of an ancestral language by the Lumbee is consistent with the widespread loss of Native American languages throughout North America. The only difference in this case is the timeframe. It stands to reason that Native American languages along the Atlantic coast, which were subjected to the encroachment of English a couple of centuries earlier than Native American languages in some western parts of North America, would have suffered ancestral language loss considerably before those in other regions. Language loss can take place very rapidly if the sociopolitical and linguistic conditions are right. In fact, it takes just a couple of generations to shift from complete proficiency in one language to another. Political and economic subjugation are prime conditions for such a shift to take place. Multilingualism can also facilitate rapid language shift. If several mutually unintelligible languages exist in a region, it encourages the learning of a common language of wider communication among groups as a lingua franca. The co-existence of different Native American languages in southeastern North Carolina at the time of the incursion of English speakers therefore would have facilitated the rapid transition to English.

We assume that there was a period in which the Lumbee knew both English and the Native language(s) and a period in which the structural features from the Native American language, called LANGUAGE TRANSFER, were still evident in the English of the Lumbee, but we cannot say exactly when these periods might have been. It is noteworthy, however, that a dialectology fieldworker from the Linguistic Atlas of the Middle and Atlantic States conducting an interview in the 1930s with a Native American who was born in Pembroke in the 1860s aborted the interview because the subject "preserves traces of the foreign speech." (Kretzschmar, McDavid, Lerud, and Johnson 1994:359). It is, of course, ironic that the accent of a Native American born of Native American parents should be referred to as "foreign" when her ancestors had inhabited the region for thousands of years before any European even knew it existed.

Reports of Native American language influence in the English of the Lumbee are also consistent with some reports by older Lumbee who spoke of their elders' use of expressions from Native American languages. So there certainly might have been vestiges of a Native American language among the Lumbee still evident in early twentieth century. There may even have been a prolonged period of bilingualism for some Lumbee through the 1800s. And if the Lumbee were indeed a conglomerate community living in a transitional Native American language zone, then some of their ancestral language would have been recorded in the documentation of Iroquoian, Siouan, and even Algonquian languages in the area.

═══════▼▼▼▼▼▼▼▼▼▼▼▼▼▼▼▼═══════ **3** ═══════▼▼▼▼▼▼▼▼▼▼▼▼▼▼▼▼═══════

THE ROOTS OF LUMBEE ENGLISH

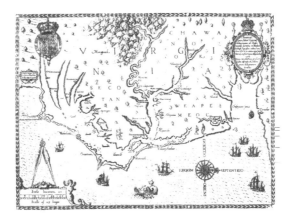

Although the Spanish and French were the first Europeans to establish colonies in the Carolinas, they appear to have had little lasting effect on the languages spoken by Native Americans in the Carolinas. The Spanish, the first Europeans to travel through North Carolina in the early to mid-sixteenth century, endeavored to establish a colony along the Carolina coast. The colony consisted of 500 men and women from the Santo Domingo region in the West Indies who brought with them slaves of African descent—reportedly the first slaves brought into America (Fernandez-Shaw 1991). However, the colony failed, and the Spanish made no other attempts to establish a colony in the Carolinas. Except for the possibility of a few names, there is no noticeable contribution of the Spanish to the language of the area. The French also led expeditions through the Carolinas in the early sixteenth century, and one of the leaders, John de Varrazano, sent a letter to King Francis I in which he noted the generosity and hospitality of the native peoples of the coastline (Hakluyt (1973: 357-60). Although neither the Spanish nor the French success-

The first Native Americans to learn English with some proficiency were probably Wanchese and Manteo from the coast of North Carolina.

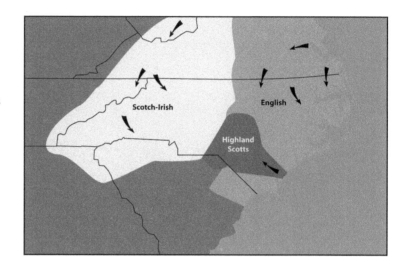

Primary locations of major European groups in North Carolina

fully colonized the North Carolina area, both groups were successful at establishing colonies in the South Carolina area.

The English, the Highland Scots, and the Scotch-Irish had the greatest influence on language development in present-day North Carolina when more widescale colonization took place. The primary locations of inhabitants from the major European groups in North Carolina and the routes of migration are indicated in the map.

The English

By the time the English had established their first successful colony in Jamestown, Virginia, in the early seventeenth century they had already made at least three other trips to the coastal regions of present-day North Carolina and Virginia. Each of these voyages is significant because there was contact between the English and the Native Americans; in some cases, the contact was fairly extensive. The first English expedition to the Americas in 1584 was led by Captains Amadas and Barlowe, who intended to survey the prospect of English colonization along the coastal regions of America. However, these explorers did not simply survey the coast and its inhabitants like others; Amadas and Barlowe took two young Native American men from coastal North

▼▼▼

Photographs by David Oxendine

Carolina, Wanchese and Manteo, back with them when they
returned to England. For almost an entire year, Wanchese and
Manteo were therefore in extensive contact with English speakers
and no doubt learned some English. They were probably the first
Native Americans to learn English with any degree of proficiency.

The second English expedition and first English attempt to
colonize was made in 1585, when a party of men principally from
the South and Southwest of England attempted to settle on
Roanoke Island. These colonists traveled extensively up and down
the North Carolina coast and into Virginia, going as far north as
present-day Norfolk. They crossed the Pamlico and Albemarle
Sounds in addition to navigating the Roanoke and Chowan Rivers
(Hariot 1971).

In 1587, Sir Walter Raleigh assembled colonists from the
South and Southwest of England a second time for an expedition
to Roanoke Island, and John White was appointed the governor.
The colonists and the Native-American group located on the
Outer Banks of the Carolinas maintained a peaceful relationship
(Hakluyt 1973) and were in regular contact in the first few months

THE ROOTS OF
LUMBEE ENGLISH

37

The lore of the Lost Colony connection is still prominent among some Lumbee.

of colonization. However, it remains a mystery as to how this relationship developed between these two groups after John White traveled back to England to replenish low provisions. When White returned from England nearly two years later, the colonists had disappeared, thus becoming the so-called Lost Colony. Their ultimate fate has inspired centuries of speculation, but there is still no archaeological or historical evidence documenting what happened to them. Whether the colonists perished, sought shelter with coastal Native Americans like the Hatteras, or blended with an interior tribe (Miller 2000) remains an open question, although a number of different groups have claimed to be linked to them. If the colonists did survive and unite with a Native American group, they no doubt would have had some impact on the language of Native Americans in North Carolina.

Although the Lost Colony connection is speculative, it is accepted by many of the Lumbee as a valid oral tradition. The belief speaks poignantly to the ethnic paradox of many Native American groups. They have been asked to provide proof of their ancestral heritage with a particular Native American ancestral language while, at the same time, being subjected to a sociopolitical system that has granted privilege on the basis of European American identity. A sense of privilege in this society would thus be most naturally achieved in the minds of some through an affinity with a European lineage, such as the Lost Colony. At the same time, Native American identity would be enhanced by a connection with a specific, historically documented coastal tribal affiliation. If nothing else, the connection between a distinct Native American group and a mysterious but celebrated British group shows how legend functions in the construction of identity.

In the final analysis, of course, it is not bloodlines, DNA, or archaeology that serves as the basis for cultural and linguistic integrity, but the construction of ethnic identity that includes cultural practices and traditions, including legends. Cultural definition is not ultimately a matter of historical documentation but a sense of self-definition and cultural practice. In this regard, it is indisputable that the Lumbee, regardless of documented historical record, have a strong sense of cultural identity and distinctiveness that sets them apart from other cultural groups in the area and beyond.

The Highlanders and Ulster Scots

Prior to 1700, the English colonists had the greatest effect on the adoption of the English language by Native Americans. The coastal areas of the Carolinas started to get regular inhabitants in the mid-1600s and particularly during the end of the 1600s and early 1700s, with some movement inward from that point. Many of the inhabitants came south from Virginia, but some came directly from the British Isles, and some even came from Caribbean areas such as Bermuda. Major immigration into North Carolina, however, did not take place until the 1700s when Scots and Scotch-Irish immigrants began their infiltration. Part of the reason for the slow colonization of North Carolina prior to this stage was due to the hazardous navigation routes and an abundance of swampland, or *pocosin*, the Algonquian term for broken or open terrain that described the topography of much of coastal Carolina.

Just before North Carolina became a royal colony in 1729, both Lowland and Highland Scots emigrated from Scotland into North Carolina. Although a few Lowland Scots colonies were established, the Highland Scots comprised the substantial majority of the immigrants and provided the most influence on the developing language varieties of the region. Highland Scots apparently migrated from the Argyll Peninsula of Western Scotland (Montgomery and Mishoe 1999) and established colonies along the North Carolina coast, just inland along the Cape Fear River, and later in the interior of Carolina in the Cape Fear River Valley. Although Highland Scots settlers would have been familiar with English, their primary language was Gaelic. In fact, Gaelic was reportedly spoken in some Carolina Highland Scots settlements up until the mid-1800s (Meyer 1961).

As Highland Scots settlements were developing and spreading into the interior regions of North Carolina, Scotch-Irish immigrants were traveling into the Piedmont area from the North. The Scotch-Irish began migration from Ulster Ireland to America in the 1600s, originally settling in Virginia, Pennsylvania, and Delaware. Within a couple of generations, the Scotch-Irish pushed west and south, settling the mountains and Piedmont of North Carolina, and the highlands of Kentucky, Tennessee, and Georgia (Montgomery 1989). Indeed, the Scotch-Irish migration was so strong between 1730-1770 that settlements stretched across most of the Southeast by the time of the Revolutionary War. The primary language of these immigrants from North Ulster would have been a distinct variety of English that is still manifested in the highland speech of Western North Carolina, or so-called Appalachian English (Wolfram and Christian 1976; Montgomery 1989; Montgomery and Hall forthcoming).

By the time that the English, the Scottish Highlanders, and the Scotch-Irish had become successful inhabitants of North Carolina and Robeson County in the early to mid 1700s, the Lumbee were apparently no longer exclusively reliant on their ancestral language for communication, at least in their interactions with outsiders (Dial and Eliades 1975). Whether or not the Lumbee originated on the coast and migrated into Robeson County or were already established as the county's original inhabitants, they would very likely have been exposed to varieties of English from the South of England, the primary regions of origin for those traveling to Virginia and North Carolina before 1700. Furthermore, this exposure could have been either direct—from the travelers and new inhabitants themselves—or indirect transmission through other Native American groups that associated with the travelers. By the close of the eighteenth century, Lumbee English might have been influenced not only by the varieties of English that these groups would have brought to Robeson County but also possibly by varieties of Gaelic and Scottish spoken in the region. Reports indicate that the Lumbee and Highland Scots did not live completely separately but associated with one another on a fairly regular basis (Evans 1971). Thus, it is not unlikely that language features from several different language backgrounds might have been shared between the groups in their early association.

African Americans

Another significant part of Robeson County is the African-American population brought to the region originally by European settlers in the mid-1700s. Although the number of slaves per household was relatively low in the region by comparison with other areas of the South (Kay and Cary 1995), varieties of African American English in Robeson County may have influenced the development of Lumbee English in some ways, especially after the turn of the nineteenth century. African Americans coming to the region would have spoken English that ranged from creole-based Gullah brought by slaves who came north from the Charleston area (Dial and Eliades 1975) to the dialects of Tidewater English brought by African Americans who came south from Virginia. Because the swampy terrain of the region was conducive for hiding, it was suited for runaway slaves, and there were free African Americans as well as slaves in the 1700s. The population of African Americans, however, was small by comparison with some large plantation areas in neighboring South Carolina. The proportion of African Americans in Robeson County has fluctuated from between a fourth to a third of the population over the last couple of centuries, not unlike that found in other Coastal Plain areas of North Carolina (Kay and Cary 1995), although questions about the reliability of demographic statistics remain because historic patterns of classification did not consistently distinguish Native Americans—"free people of color"—from other non-Whites.

The social relations between the Lumbee and African Americans, as well as with other ethnic groups, have naturally shifted over time. It has been reported, for example, that prior to the nineteenth century, a degree of egalitarianism between the Lumbee and the Scotch-Irish and Highland Scots groups existed (Evans 1971). If this was in fact true, the nature of this relationship changed drastically over time, particularly after the passage of the Revised State Constitution of 1835, which mandated that people of color did not have the rights and privileges afforded those who were White. Rights and privileges that the Lumbee might have appropriated prior to the nineteenth century were therefore stripped away by government fiat. Moreover, this legislation effectively deprived the Lumbee of official recognition as Indian through the census; instead, they were grouped with other people of color. The early nineteenth century thus marked the onset of a new kind of status for the Lumbee in which they were classified with other people of color, in particular, African Americans. Such a classification also would have an essential effect on how they defined themselves in relation to other groups since privilege now came though affiliation with the dominant White group—from whom they now were legally disenfranchised. Their legal classification with people of color would serve to motivate a disassociation from African Americans, the primary target of the legislation. In an important sense, the Lumbee were caught between Whites and Blacks. But such an ambiguous status also may have helped to perpetuate a sense of "otherness" apart from both groups.

Henry Berry Lowrie's house as it appeared at its original site a few miles from Pembroke. It has now been moved to the North Carolina Indian Cultural Center.

Subordinate ethnic status, cultural isolation, and oppression by Europeans are an important background for understanding the development of Lumbee English. The sociopolitical situation subjugated non-European groups to European intruders, but its backlash may have also served to create a strong sense of cultural cohesion and foster ethnic solidarity. Historically, the Lumbee have endured acts of discrimination based on their non-White status, and reports of violence, segregation in the school and workplace, and unequal power relations in county government are still recounted vividly by many Lumbee. But in the face of such oppression, particular historical events also demonstrate a Lumbee commitment to stand up against acts of oppression and terrorism. In fact, these events have come to play an important role in the Lumbee historical tradition.[2]

[2] The two most prominent examples of such incidents are the well-publicized Lowrie insurrection (1865-1872), which featured a group of Lumbees who fought against the tyranny of Whites (Farris 1925; Evans 1971), and the Lumbee confrontation of a Ku Klux Klan rally in 1958 (Evans 1971). Practically all Lumbees are familiar with the Lowrie rebellion led by Henry Berry Lowrie, who is now accorded Robin Hood-like stature by many in the historical tradition of the Lumbee. The Lumbee confrontation of the Ku Klux Klan a century later again illustrated their unified strength and group resolve when confronted with acts of attempted repression and intimidation. Perhaps as much as the historical incidents themselves, these documented episodes point to a strong and persistent sense of determination in the face of external threats to their sense of peoplehood. In both of these incidents, it is the Lumbee as a people who served notice that they would stand up against those who attempted to strip them of their dignity.

THE ROOTS OF
LUMBEE ENGLISH

43

Many local stores in Pembroke highlight Native American themes.

Photograph by Neal Hutcheson

Evidence also suggests that the relationships between the Lumbee and the African Americans and European Americans are not constant and have varied widely over time, group, and individual. For example, before they petitioned for funds to create their own schools staffed with Native American teachers, the Lumbee who went to school attended schools with either European Americans or African Americans. After the State government granted funds and the Lumbee community developed its own school, however, Lumbee students were educated only with other Lumbee, and this segregated schooling lasted in some instances until legal desegregation in the early 1970s. Since the 1970s, the schools have been more mixed, even though *de facto* segregation still exists on many levels.

At certain periods in history, some Lumbee worked outside of the county for extensive periods of time. In the nineteenth and early half of the twentieth century, for example, Native Americans and European Americans alike apparently worked in the turpentine and logging industries. This required extensive periods of absence and traveling throughout the South. Indeed, the insularity of the Lumbee in Robeson County is quite relative and has shifted over time based on social, historical, and political circumstances within and outside the community. And different Lumbee groups and individuals have been more or less insular, depending on their status within the community and their social relations within and outside of the community. This kind of fluctuation cannot be ignored in describing the past, current, and future state of the English used by groups of and individual Lumbee speakers.

4

THE DEVELOPMENT OF LUMBEE ENGLISH

Courtesy of Indian Education Resource Center

How did Lumbee English develop its distinctive dialect traits? Are there any vestiges of a heritage Native American language still evident in the dialect? How does it compare with other dialects of American English—including the dialects of European Americans and African Americans in the immediate area and other historically isolated regions of North Carolina? Is there any indication that the dialect might be linked to the language spoken by residents of the Outer Banks, one of the possible sites of earlier contact with English speakers?

A resurgent interest in traditional arts and crafts characterizes the contemporary Lumbee community.

Language researchers, particularly the staff of the North Carolina Language and Life Project, have been attempting to answer some of these questions based on several kinds of language information. First, linguists have conducted interviews with Robeson County residents of all ages and ethnicities. Over the past decade, fieldworkers from the North Carolina Language and Life Project have interviewed more than 100 Lumbee in Robeson County who ranged in age from 10 through 96; they have also interviewed about 50 European Americans and 25 African

Sisters Ashley and Casey Matthews underscore the important role of family in Lumbee life.

Americans in Robeson County in order to make comparisons across different ethnic groups. Most of these interviews include 45-90 minutes of conversation about topics of interest to the participants. Each of these interviews has been listened to in minute detail to document examples of particular dialect structures.

There are additional tape-recorded interviews available for linguistic analysis, including several oral history projects. For example, Adolph Dial conducted a series of oral history interviews in 1969-1971, and these offer a good repository for language as well as history, as do interviews conducted by various students with their parents and grandparents. There are also other oral history interviews with the Lumbee conducted in the late 1960s and early 1970s available in an oral history collection formerly housed at the University of Florida but now available in Pembroke. In addition to these repositories, university students, including several students from Robeson County (e.g. Atkinson 1995; Jackson 1996; Hammonds 2000; Kerns 2001), have conducted research projects on particular topics related to Lumbee English. A list of articles, theses, and dissertations related to Lumbee English is found in the appendix.

Earlier recordings are of particular interest since they provide a historical perspective on the development of Lumbee speech. An 80 year-old speaker interviewed in 1970 would reflect what Lumbee English might have been like when the speaker learned language in the late nineteenth century, since speakers tend to retain many features of the dialect they learned as a child. The earliest records of speech we have, in fact, include speakers who were born in the 1860s, giving a time-depth of well over a century. Such time depth is essential in order to see how the dialect has changed over time and how it is currently developing.

One of the most frequently asked questions is whether there are any traces of a heritage Native American language in present-day Lumbee English. The reasoning behind this question seems apparent: if influence from a Native American language is found in Lumbee English it might lead us to the ancestral language of the

Many objects in Pembroke bear the image of Lumbee culture.

Lumbee while, at the same time, it would authenticate Native American lineage for those in search of such evidence. Such a hopeful expectation, however, is balanced by a couple of practical observations. Although American English has certainly adopted some terms from Native American languages in the course of its development—for example, words such as *pocosin*, *chipmunk*, *opossum*, and so forth, are derived from different Native American languages—the overall influence of Native American languages on American English has not been substantial. Place names are the exception, and there are hundreds of names in the Eastern United States alone that are derived from Native American words. Sometimes, these place names give important clues to the Native American languages present in the area, as Rudes (forthcoming) suggests for North Carolina. For obvious political reasons, borrowing from other European languages was much more rampant in the development of the dialects of American English than borrowing from Native American languages (*Dictionary of American Regional English* 1986, 1991, 1996).

It must be noted further that vestiges of influence from a heritage language can disappear in a hurry. Consider how quickly children of parents whose first language is a language other than English may shift to monolingual English in the United States.

THE DEVELOPMENT
OF LUMBEE ENGLISH

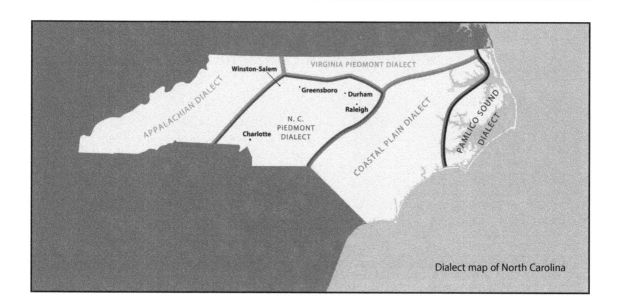

Dialect map of North Carolina

The parents may speak heavily accented English and struggle to converse in English but the children show no influences from their parents' language in their English, and the grandchildren may not have any knowledge of the heritage language at all. It is not unusual for linguistic influence from an ancestral language to vanish completely in a couple of generations, so that it stands to reason that no Native American language influence would persist a number of generations after the heritage language was no longer used. It would be quite surprising to find lingering influence from an ancestral language given the relatively early shift to English by the Lumbee.

One possible exception to this general finding, however, is presented in an article by Torbert (2001), whose highly detailed analysis of the pronunciation of final consonants in words like *find*, *rest*, and *act* uncovers a trend that might point to lingering vestiges of heritage language influence in Lumbee English. In a careful, quantitative examination of the absence of the final consonant, for example, pronouncing *find* as *fin'*, *rest* as *res'*, or *act* as *ac'*, Torbert found that Lumbee speakers born before World War I are more prone to leave off the final consonant than those born in the mid and later twentieth century. This reduction of final consonant combinations at the ends of words is a fairly typical holdover effect in English where the native language does not have these types of consonant combinations, and has been documented in the English of Native American communities elsewhere (Wolfram 1980; Leap 1993; Wolfram, Childs, and Torbert 2000). Although it is a very subtle dimension of language that would not be very noticeable to the ordinary listener, it is not unreasonable to attribute this pronunciation tendency among the oldest speakers of Lumbee English to the holdover effects of ancestral language influence. Certainly, we would not expect to find the effects of a language lost generations ago to be prominently displayed, but the possibility of subtle lingering effects cannot be dismissed.

Creating Lumbee English

The substance of Lumbee English has clearly been molded out of the varieties of English made available through contacts with English groups of various types. To begin with, a couple of dialect traits show a connection with Outer Banks English. Perhaps the most obvious case is the pronunciation of the vowel in *time* and *side* like *toim* and *soid* by older speakers in communities such as Prospect and Union Chapel (Schilling-Estes 2000), but there are other similarities as well. The use of *weren't* in sentences such as *I weren't there* or *She weren't nice* is also a prominent Outer Banks feature. In fact, studies of the dialect areas of North Carolina before the 1880s (Kretzschmar et al. 1994) show that the dialect now associated with the Outer Banks once extended into the mainland area of southeastern North Carolina. While the current dialect profile has changed somewhat (see map on page 50), the dialect boundaries that emerge from earlier records are still evident today.

It might be tempting to conclude that the dialect connection with the Outer Banks supports a Lost Colony origin for the English of the Lumbee, but the facts are much more complex than this simple hypothesis. The dialect associated with Outer Banks speech was not formed until the early 1700s at the earliest, when English

settlements from Maryland and eastern Virginia traveled down the coast by water and established permanent residence along the Outer Banks and coast of North Carolina. That was well over a century after the disappearance of the Lost Colony. It must also be understood that many of the dialect features of the Outer Banks are shared not only with Lumbee English, but with other dialects that preserve earlier features of English because of geographic and cultural isolation. In this respect, the island dialects on the coast have more in common with the mountain dialects in the western part of the state than the intervening Piedmont area, but not because of their historical connection. Instead, they shared a type of isolation that fosters the retention of some of these earlier forms. For example, the use of the prefix *a-*, pronounced as an *uh* sound as in *She was a-fishin'*, is a well-documented structure of Lumbee English, Appalachian Speech, and Outer Banks speech. In this instance, the different dialects simply share the preservation of an older structure. These forms are referred to as RELIC FORMS because they are retained in traditional dialects while receding in contemporary, mainstream dialects. Another relic form is the use of *be* as a helping verb where other dialects use *have*, particularly in sentences such as *I'm been there* for *I've been there*. In the English version of the Bible translated in the early 1600s, for example, there are many constructions such as *destructions are come* for *destructions have come* or *their memorial is perished* for *their memorial has perished* (Psalms 9:6). However, it would be wrong to conclude that these forms in Lumbee English are simply static vestiges of earlier English; language is always undergoing change. Thus, while retaining some earlier uses of *be* for *have*, Lumbee English now uses it in ways it was not used originally. For example, *I'm* is now used in sentences where it is not the equivalent to *have*, as in sentences like *I'm forgot it yesterday*.

Some of the surrounding English dialects of the area also influenced the development of Lumbee English. The use of *bes* in sentences such as *Sometimes it bes that way* or *Dogs bes doing that* was apparently prominent in a region that included Robeson County and some of the surrounding counties in the vicinity, such as Horry County to the south (Montgomery and Mishoe 1999). It was particularly prominent among descendants of the Highland Scots, and can still be found in use by elderly Scottish-heritage residents of Robeson County. However, it has receded among Scottish descendants in Robeson County while remaining quite robust, and even intensifying its use in Lumbee English over the past couple of generations.

It is also possible that contact with African Americans has influenced the development of Lumbee English to some extent since both the Lumbee and African Americans have been residents of Robeson County for several centuries and, at various points in their history, they have been subjugated to similar socially subordinate roles. For example, the absence of the verb *be* in sentences such as *You nice* or *She gonna go there*, a well-known feature of African American English, is also present to some extent in Lumbee English (Dannenberg 2000). This feature has usually been attributed to a vestige of African language influence

A canoe found in the nearby Lumbee River. It has been carbon-dated to be about 1,000 years old. The canoe is on permanent display at the Museum of the Native American Resource Center.

(Rickford 1999) although it might have derived from Native American language influence as well (Leap 1993). There is, after all, African influence in Southern English, as manifested in words like *cooter* for *turtle* (probably related to the Bambara or Malinké word *kuta* 'turtle'), *catawampus* (*katakankula* 'hang unevenly'), and *bozo* (*boza* 'stumblebum'). So African American English may have also had some effect on the development of Lumbee English.

It seems clear that several different varieties of English have provided input into the development of Lumbee English over the course of its development, not only in its past but also in its present form. At the same time, Lumbee English also developed on its own, apart from any input from surrounding dialects. This is true for some dialect words that refer to social distinctions within the community—for example, the use of the term *Lum, brickhouse Indian, on the swamp*, and so forth—as well as some grammatical and pronunciation features. The grammatical construction *weren't* in *I weren't there* seems to be developing of its own accord within the community and is becoming more robust among some younger speakers. Although the precise contributions of various sources to the development of Lumbee English cannot be calculated, it is apparent that a particular set of donor language varieties available in the area combined with the dynamics of Lumbee language adaptation and innovation to forge a distinct variety of English. The development of Lumbee English is therefore no different from other sociocultural or regional varieties of English that have emerged in the United States and throughout the world, though the particular language features set it apart from other varieties.

5

THE DIALECT CONTEXT OF LUMBEE ENGLISH

Photograph by Neal Hutcheson

Although Lumbee English is certainly a distinct dialect, no dialect stands alone. Lumbee English shares features with a full range of dialects in the Carolinas and elsewhere—from mainstream, standard English to major regional, social, and ethnic vernacular varieties. To situate Lumbee English with respect to other dialects, we compare it with some of the prominent dialects in the region, ranging from Appalachian English in the mountains to Outer Banks English on the coast. Fortunately, dialectologists have carried out a number of studies of these dialects over the past several decades that allow for a convenient comparison (Wolfram and Christian 1976; Christian, Wolfram, and Dube 1988, Montgomery 1989, Montgomery and Hall forthcoming; Wolfram and Schilling-Estes 1997; Wolfram, Hazen, and Schilling-Estes 1999). For European American and African American vernacular dialects in Robeson County we rely on the analysis of speech samples collected by the North Carolina Language and Life Project over the past decade; some of the current analyses of Lumbee English routinely compare the speech of the Lumbee with

Lumbee English shares dialect features with Appalachian English to the west and Outer Banks English to the east, but the combination of dialect forms makes Lumbee speech distinct from any other variety of American English.

the speech of European American and African American cohort groups in Robeson County (e.g. Atkinson 1997; Jackson 1998; Dannenberg and Wolfram 1998; Wolfram and Sellers 1999; Dannenberg 2000).

Like all dialects, Lumbee English is distinguished on different levels, including pronunciation, grammar, and lexicon. At its core, Lumbee English is a Southern regional dialect, sharing many widespread features of Southern speech. However, it tends to compare more favorably with geographically and socially isolated groups—such as those in the mountains and on the coast—than it does with the Southern speech found in the Piedmont and Coastal Plain. Thus, many visitors hearing the dialect for the first time think that it sounds like Appalachian English or Outer Banks English. While outsiders think of it as sounding distinctive and not quite like any dialect they have heard, they do not necessarily associate it with a distinctive Native American variety. In fact, when we gave the speech samples of Lumbee English, African American English, and European American English discussed in Chapter 1 to a group of 40 listeners in Raleigh, North Carolina, located about 100 miles north of Robeson County, we got quite different patterns of ethnic identification. The listeners, who for the most part knew who the Lumbee were but did not know much about them, were unable to distinguish them reliably from European Americans and African Americans. In fact, their correct identification of the Lumbee speakers was only 39 percent, which amounted to a random choice given three options for their answer. This contrasted significantly with the 80 percent correct identification rate indicated by Robeson County listeners (Wolfram 2000). By contrast, the Raleigh group identified African Americans from Robeson County correctly over 90 percent of the time and the Robeson County European Americans correctly 80 percent of the time. In the vast majority of the cases where Lumbee English was misidentified (over 75 percent), the listeners identified it as White speech, suggesting that it shares more prominent dialect features with Southern European American English than with African American English.

What do these kinds of findings say about the dialect context of Lumbee English? They suggest that the cultural identity of Lumbee English as a sociocultural variety is a fairly local one. In the tri-ethnic context of Robeson County, where residents are highly aware of three distinct sociocultural groups, there is a strong awareness of the dialects associated with these groups. But outside of this area, the dialect game is different. Most Americans, particularly in the South, think of ethnic speech solely in terms of a bi-racial dichotomy—as either Black or White—and they have a difficult time relating to other types of ethnic speech distinctions. But Lumbee English defies the stereotypical notions of ethnic speech. Accordingly, outside listeners have trouble figuring out where Lumbee English fits, both ethnically and regionally. Listeners who become familiar with the Lumbee situation in the context of Robeson County, however, have quite different reactions: they have little difficulty assigning speech to one of the three significant cultural groups of the region. In other words, the more knowledgeable a person becomes about the Lumbee community in the context of southeastern North Carolina, the more significant speech becomes as an emblem of cultural heritage.

A Dialect Comparison

A number of the descriptive linguistic studies of Lumbee English focus on single dialect structures in great technical detail (Wolfram 1996, Dannenberg and Wolfram 1998; Wolfram and Sellers 1999; Dannenberg 1999, 2000, 2002; Torbert 2001). Although it is sometimes difficult for linguists to discuss dialect structures without paying attention to minute structural detail, that is not the intention in this comparison. Instead, we simply aim to highlight some major features of Lumbee English compared with other dialects without getting lost in technical linguistic description. It is important, however, to keep in mind the extensive and expanding technical research database for the descrip-

Photograph by Neal Hutcheson

tion. It may be surprising to find over 50 pages of printed text devoted to a single construction such as *I'm* in sentences like *I'm been there* in Lumbee English (Wolfram 1996; Dannenberg 2002), but this is often what it takes to describe the peculiar history, development and current use of this form.

It is possible to compare Lumbee English with other dialects in terms of vocabulary, pronunciation, and grammar. Perhaps the most obvious level is vocabulary, where different words are used for the same object or have different nuances of meaning. Most popular descriptions focus on the words of Lumbee English, and some word uses and phrases seem quite distinctive. However, words and phrases can also be a lot more complex than they appear at first glance, with overlapping uses and meaning nuances that subtly distinguish dialects. Words can also be stubbornly independent in their development and dialectologists are fond of saying that "each word has its own history."

First, there is a limited set of unique Lumbee words. Some of these are local innovations for places and social relations that have arisen within the community, such as *on the swamp*, a metaphorical extension of the swampy terrain. Many proper name locations include swamp in their name: *Burnt Swamp*, *Hog Swamp*, *Ashpole Swamp*, *Gum Swamp*, *Saddletree Swamp*, and so forth. The term

Lum, a familiar form of Lumbee, is reserved for those who have identified with their Lumbee cultural heritage; it also indicates a sense of community and peoplehood that distinguishes the Lumbee from other groups, and therefore is significant in designating insider-outsider status. As is often the case in culturally distinct communities, social designations are also embodied in some of the vocabulary items. The term *daddy*, for example, is used for close peer friends as well as a parent, and teenagers may greet one another with "What's up, Daddy." The term *cuz*, shortened from *cousin*, is similar in its extension of a kinship term to refer to good friends. Social distinctions within the community are captured by terms like *brickhouse Indian* and *swamp Indian*, which refer to higher and lower status in the community; these are combined with the common Southern term *above your raisin's* to refer to someone who "puts on airs." The fact that a number of the unique Lumbee terms refer to social relations within the community, including extended kinship, says a great deal about the internal social structure. Other terms, such as *fine in the world* 'doing well' and *sorry in the world* 'doing badly' or 'not feeling well' or *ellick* for 'coffee' (usually with sugar) also separate the Lumbee community from other communities.

Some lexical items indicate a shared but restricted regional pattern. For example, the term *kelvinator* is a brand name for refrigerator that has been extended to refer to refrigerators in general because a Kelvinator factory once existed in the area. Thus, all ethnic groups within the region simply extended the proper name to include all refrigerators, just as people in other areas use the term *frigidaire* for refrigerators in general. The term *juvember* for slingshot is probably used more by the Lumbee than by other residents of Robeson County, but it is also used by other groups in Southeastern North Carolina. The term *cooter* for turtle is a local term that is shared by African Americans and the Lumbee, apparently derived by the Lumbee from their African American neighbors who retained the term from their African language heritage.

THE DIALECT CONTEXT
OF LUMBEE ENGLISH

Another set of words shows the longstanding resemblance of Lumbee English to other isolated groups outside of the immediate vicinity, thus indicating a kind of long-term effect from some of the earliest English inhabitants. For example, terms like *mommuck*, *toten*, and *gaum*, which can be traced back centuries in the English language, have been retained in Lumbee English just as they have in other geographically and culturally isolated groups to the east and west of the Lumbee. However, some subtle shifts in meaning have taken place in the different regions. Thus, *mommuck*, which is well documented in the plays of Shakespeare, had an original, literal meaning of 'tear to shreds' during the 1600s. On the Outer Banks, this meaning has been extended figuratively to mean 'harass physically or mentally' as in *Stop mommucking me*, while in Lumbee English and in Appalachian English to the west, its meaning has been extended to mean 'make a mess', as in *You sure mommucked the house*. The common etymological origin of this word has been subjected to slight shifts in meaning that now subtly define its use in the different dialect communities while reflecting its archaic status. The term *token*, which can be traced back a millennium in the English language, is another relic form that has undergone a shift in meaning. In Lumbee English, where it is often pronounced as *toten*, it refers to a spirit or ghost; it can also refer to a sign or foreshadowing of death, as it does on the Outer Banks of North Carolina (Wolfram and Schilling-Estes 1997).

Finally, there is a large set of more general vocabulary items that Lumbee English shares with a wide range of Southern English dialects. Uses of *mash* for 'push' and *cut off/on* for 'turn on/off' as in *We mashed the button to cut on the lights* are fairly widespread Southern uses that set apart Southern varieties of English from non-Southern dialects. Similarly, terms like *swanny* for swear, *carry* for accompany, *young 'uns* for children, and so forth are simply words that define a broad-based area of the South, including the major ethnic groups in Robeson County. Lumbee English vocabulary exists within the general context of Southern speech while setting itself apart in a few but significant ways.

Cross-Dialectal Comparison of Lexical Items

Lexical Item	Lumbee English	Robeson Eur.-Am. English	Robeson Af.-Am. English	Appal. English	Outer Banks English
Lum 'Lumbee person'	✓				
on the swamp 'in the neighborhood'	✓				
brickhouse Indian 'upper class'	✓				
ellick 'coffee'	✓				
sorry in the world 'badly'	✓				
juvember 'sling shot'	✓	✓	(✓)		
kelvinator 'refrigerator'	✓	✓	✓		
chawed 'embarrassed'	✓	✓		✓	
kernal 'swelling'	✓	✓		✓	
jubious 'eerie', 'strange'	✓			✓	
gaum 'mess'	✓	✓		✓	
toten 'sign of spirit or ghost'	✓			✓	✓
mommuck 'mess'	✓			✓	✓
cooter 'turtle'	✓	(✓)	✓		
tote 'carry'	✓	✓	✓	✓	✓
swanny 'swear'	✓	✓	✓	✓	✓
carry 'accompany, escort'	✓	✓	✓	✓	✓
young 'uns 'children'	✓	✓	✓	✓	✓
mash 'push'	✓	✓	✓	✓	✓

THE DIALECT CONTEXT
OF LUMBEE ENGLISH

A sample comparison of some vocabulary items is summarized in the table. In order to place Lumbee English in an appropriate comparative context, several different dialects are included. These include Robeson County African American Vernacular English and European American Vernacular English, as well as two other historically isolated varieties in the more expansive region, Outer Banks English and Appalachian English. The examination of Lumbee English in this broader context gives insight into both the historical and current relations of Lumbee English with other Southern dialects. The items in the table come from more extensive dialect comparisons such as Locklear et al. (1999) and Barton (n.d.) for Lumbee English; Wolfram and Schilling-Estes (1997) for Outer Banks English; and Montgomery and Hall (forthcoming) for Appalachian English in the Smoky Mountain region. A check ✓ means that the word is found in this particular variety; in a few cases, parentheses around the (✓) indicate that the item is found but to a very limited degree. In some cases, different dialects may share a word but its level of usage is much more prominent in one dialect and there might be different nuances in its meaning.

This limited comparison of vocabulary among Lumbee speakers in Robeson County reveals the overlapping yet distinctive base of the dialect—both in respect to other ethnic dialects in the immediate area and in respect to other culturally and geographically insulated varieties in the Southern mountains and coastal islands. Although there is a relatively small set of words and phrases used only by the Lumbee, some of these are very symbolic of the internal social structure of the Lumbee community.

Dialect Pronunciation

The pronunciation patterns of Lumbee English follow Southern dialects of English in the Coastal Plain of the South, although the mix of these features with other traits characteristic of historically isolated dialects tends to makes its pronunciation distinct from other dialects in the immediate region. We already mentioned the pronunciation of the long ī sound of words like *time* or *side*, one of the most distinctive sounds associated with the development of the South. Older speakers in more traditional Lumbee communities such as Prospect and Union Chapel may still pronounce these vowels like *toim* or *soid*, the pronunciation strongly associated with the Outer Banks. The more common present-day Southern pronunciation of this vowel, however, is without the glide, so that *time* is pronounced as *tahm* and *side* as *sahd*. This is the trend found among younger Lumbee, which aligns them with the speech of European Americans and African Americans in Robeson County. However, a detailed analysis of the pronunciation of this vowel over four different generations of Lumbee speakers (born before World War I, born between World War I and World War II, born after World War II but before school integration in 1972, and born after school integration) shows that there are still some subtle ways in which this vowel is differentiated on the basis of ethnicity (Schilling-Estes 2000). Whereas speakers from all Robeson County ethnic groups unglide the vowel of *time* and *side*, younger Lumbee speakers are more likely to unglide the vowel in words like *light* and *bright* so that they are pronounced as *laht* and *braht*, thus distinguishing them from the other ethnic groups. Such a realignment shows how Lumbee English may shift over time while still maintaining ethnic distinctions.

Such cases also point to the subtle distinctions that fine-grained linguistic analysis can sometimes reveal—differences that are not always immediately apparent to the ear of the casual listener. For example, some of these phonetic distinctions only emerge when extensive quantitative analysis and instrumental analysis of sound waves are conducted. In some cases, differences are manifested when a large number of examples from conversational speech samples is extracted and subjected to technical statistical analysis (Miller 1996; Wolfram and Sellers 1999; Dannenberg 2000; Schilling-Estes 2000). The analysis of *r-* loss in words like *fouh* for *four* or *feuh* for *fear* is one of those cases where qualitative comparisons do not reveal the subtle ethnic distinc-

Researcher Benjamin Torbert measures the sound waves of Lumbee vowels using the Computerized Speech Laboratory.

The Dialect Context of Lumbee English

tions. Robeson County is considered to be a transitional zone with respect to the loss of *r* after a vowel, and the *r* may or may not be present. Although speakers from the three major ethnic groups of Robeson County exhibit *r*-loss, the careful measurement of hundreds of cases shows that the relative level of *r*-loss is different. Thus, two different studies (Miller 1996; Dannenberg 1997) confirm that the relative incidence of *r*-loss in words like *cah* for *car* and *feuh* for *fear* is the highest for Robeson County African American speakers and lowest for Robeson County European Americans. Lumbee speakers fall in between, distinguishing themselves quantitatively from both groups. Another study (Schilling-Estes 1998) shows that the differences in *r*-loss are even subtler, as speakers adjust their levels of *r*-loss based on the person they are talking to, what they are talking about, and the kinds of relationships that speakers have to each other.

Modern computerized methods of phonetic analysis also help reveal the significant distinctions in vowel systems. For example, it is now possible to use computer programs that measure the precise production of vowels based on the physics of sound waves, so-called vowel formants. This kind of acoustic analysis can be applied to any vowel taken from a tape recording of natural conversation—for example, the individual vowels of *time*, *boat*, *beet*, *fat*, and so forth. Each vowel is isolated from the stream of conversation using the computerized program, and the sound waves for the vowel are systematically measured in Hertz. The scores are then automatically plotted on a graph showing where the vowels are produced in the speaker's mouth. Such fine-grained analysis allows the analyst to make precise, detailed comparisons of overall vowel systems. Analysis of this type for the vowel system of Robeson County Lumbee, European-Americans, and African Americans by Thomas (2001) has been instrumental in arriving at the conclusion that the Lumbee English vowel system is more like that of Robeson County European American speakers than it is like Robeson County African Americans (Thomas 2001:197-198). The results of the acoustic analysis may also help explain one of the results of the listener identification test that showed that the Lumbee who are misidentified in terms of ethnicity are categorized as White rather than African American.

As we already pointed out, the vernacular version of Lumbee English often shows an affinity with the traditional dialects of geographically and socially isolated dialects such as Appalachian English and the Outer Banks English. For example, the retention of an *h* in words like *hit* for *it* or *hain't* for *ain't*, the intrusion of a *t* in *oncet*, *twicet*, or *clifft*, and the use of the plural *–es* with words like *postes* for *posts*, *roastes* for *roasts*, or even *woodses* for *woods*, are characteristic of isolated varieties in regions quite removed from the area now occupied by the Lumbee. The connection between these dialects is further strengthened by the pronunciation of the final *r* in *yeller* for *yellow* or *feller* for *fellow*, *right here* as *right chere*, and *young 'uns* for *young ones* or *second 'un* for *second one*. The table compares some pronunciation features of Lumbee English with other relevant vernacular dialects.

The comparison shows that there is very little about the pronunciation of words in Lumbee English that is unique. At its core, it is connected with the traditional dialects of the South, but it often has more in common with the dialects of the Outer Banks and Appalachia than it does with some of dialects of non-Lumbee residents within Robeson County. When the various pronunciation

Cross-Dialectal Comparison of Pronunciation Features

Pronunciation Feature	Lumbee English	Robeson Eur.-Am. English	Robeson Af.-Am. English	Appal. English	Outer Banks English
ī vowel as oi: e.g. *time* as *toim: side* as *soid*	✓				✓
ī ungliding before voiceless sounds e.g. *light* as *laht; right* as *raht*	✓			✓	
ī ungliding before voiced sounds e.g. *time* as *tahm; side* as *sahd*	✓	✓	✓	✓	
h retention e.g. *it* as *hit; hain't* as *ain't*	✓			✓	✓
ea before r: e.g. *there* as *thar; bear* as *bar*	✓			✓	✓
intrusive t e.g. *once* as *oncet; cliff* as *clifft*	✓			✓	✓
long -es plural e.g. *posts* as *postes* *roast* as *roastes*	✓			✓	✓
ng as nk e.g. *anything* as *anythink*	✓			(✓)	(✓)
ch for t before y or ee e.g. *right here* as *rightch here*	✓			✓	(✓)
final r for ow e.g. *fellow* as *feller* *yellow* as *yeller*	✓	(✓)		✓	✓
ire reduction e.g. *fire* as *far; tire* as *tar*	✓	✓		✓	✓
initial w loss e.g. *young ones* as *young 'uns*	✓	✓	(✓)	✓	✓
merger of i and e before n e.g. *pen* as *pin*	✓	✓	✓	✓	✓
r- loss after a vowel e.g. *fear* as *feuh; four* as *fouh*	(✓)	(✓)	✓		

The Dialect Context
of Lumbee English

elements are combined, it is usually identifiable as Lumbee—especially to those who live in the general vicinity of Robeson County.

Sentence Structure

Perhaps the most intriguing part of Lumbee English is its sentence structure, or grammar. Although the overwhelming majority of grammatical features in Lumbee English are once again shared with other English dialects, there are several features that are distinctly Lumbee in the context of Southeastern North Carolina. As with pronunciation, Lumbee English aligns itself with the dialects of historically remote regions such as those on the Outer Banks and in Appalachia. For example, *a*- prefixing in constructions such as *She was a-huntin' and a-fishin'* is a fairly common relic form of English found in historically isolated rural dialects. While this form is receding in Lumbee English, as it is in other dialects, it does not seem to be vanishing quite as rapidly as it is in these other areas. Another feature now diminishing is the use of an *-s* on verbs in sentences like *The dogs barks* or *People bes like that*. Technically, this involves the attachment of the suffix *-s* to a verb when it occurs with a plural subject. In standard English, of course, the *–s* attaches to the verb only when it the subject is singular, as in *The dog barks*. This pattern of *–s* on verbs with plural subjects, which came from North of England and Scotch-Irish from Ulster, was fairly widespread in colonial American English; it is also documented in most remote regions in the South where some older forms of English have been preserved. It is, for example, commonly used in Appalachia and on the Outer Banks, and can also be found among some older European American residents of Scottish heritage in Robeson County. It is not found in the neighboring African American community, where the absence of the *–s* on all verbs is more typical, as in *She go* for *She goes*. Some vernacular speakers of Lumbee English may use the *–s* with subjects other than third person as well in *You gets you a wife* or *I thinks it's nice* but this pattern is no longer very pervasive.

Although a number of features in present-day Lumbee English are relics of structures once well-represented in English, some are now associated mainly with the Lumbee in the context of Southeastern North Carolina. One of these is the use of *be* where other dialects use *have*, as in *I'm been there before* for *I've been there before*. Lumbee English may use sentences such as *I'm been there* or *We're got it already* where other dialects would use *have* as in *I've been there already* or *We've got it already*. This use is an apparent vestige of an earlier period in the English language when *be* and *have* alternated in this way (Wolfram 1996). This use of *be* in perfect tense constructions is still found in insular, English-speaking communities as far removed as Samaná English in the Dominican Republic (Tagliamonte 1997), loyalists from the Carolinas who settled in the Bahamas (Sellers 1999), and in the world's most isolated inhabited island, Tristan da Cunha in the South Atlantic (Schreier 2001). So the form itself is hardly unique to Lumbee English. What is distinct about it is the fact that this use has become so strongly associated with the Lumbee in Robeson County; it is rarely if ever used by comparable local groups of European American and African Americans. We thus see how Lumbee English took advantage of the available English language resources and crafted them into a distinct cultural variety.

The verb *be* in the past tense also distinguishes Lumbee English from other dialects in the area. *Be* is the most irregular verb in English, having several different forms in the present tense (*am, are, is*) and two past tense forms (*was, were*). Since it is so irregular in its structure, there is a natural tendency among vernacular dialects throughout the English-speaking world to REGU-

LARIZE, that is, reduce its use to one variant with all subjects. In most cases, this is the form *was* so that a vernacular dialect will simply use *I/you/she/they/you/they was there*. But Lumbee English, along with Outer Banks English, is one of the few dialects in the United States to use a different pattern. In this pattern, the regularized form in negative sentences is *weren't*, so that speakers will say *I weren't, she weren't, it weren't* and so forth. In Robeson County, this use seems to be largely restricted to the Lumbee. Other dialects in the region may use a form that sounds something like *weren't*, as in *I won't there* or *She won't there* for *I wasn't there* or *She wasn't there*, but this use is really quite different (Schilling-Estes and Wolfram 1994; Wolfram and Sellers 1999; Hazen 1998). Once again, the grammatical structure demonstrates an intriguing similarity between Lumbee English and Outer Banks English. No other dialect of English this far inland has maintained this pattern, although it remains quite robust in island and coastal dialects that extend from the southern portion of the Outer Banks of North Carolina to the island communities in the Chesapeake Bay of Virginia and Maryland to the north.

One other grammatical structure shows how Lumbee English has molded forms derived from the dialects made available to them in its earlier, formative period. This is the form *be(s)* in sentences

The train depot was an important building and place for the Lumbee community.

THE DIALECT CONTEXT
OF LUMBEE ENGLISH

such as *She bes here* or *Sometimes babies bes born like that* (Dannenberg and Wolfram 1998). This use of *be* where other dialects use *is* or *are* apparently dates back to early Highland Scots and the Scotch-Irish English influence on the dialects of the region; in fact, this use of *be* has been documented in neighboring European American varieties (Montgomery and Mishoe 1999). Although it is now rare in European American varieties in Robeson County, it is still prominent in Lumbee English. At the same time that *bes* shows an apparent relationship to Scots and Scotch-Irish dialects prominent in the area historically, it also accommodates a similar form in African American Vernacular English, namely, the so-called 'habitual *be*' in sentences such as *Sometimes she be going to the store* or *They be taking the dog with them all the time*. In contemporary African American Vernacular English, the form *be* occurs with verb constructions such as *be talking, be tripping,* and so forth, to indicate activities that take place habitually—that is, repeated actions. Among Lumbee speakers, particularly younger speakers, it is being modified in the direction of the African American English use, but it remains subtly distinct in a couple of ways. In Lumbee English, *be* can take the *-s* suffix, as *It bes like that* whereas in African American Vernacular English it usually occurs without an *-s*, as in *She be_ talking*. Also, some speakers of Lumbee English still preserve the use of *be* for *have* as in *She be got it* for *She has got it* or *I might be lost some inches* for *I have lost some inches*. These uses are not found in African American Vernacular English. Lumbee Vernacular English is thus distinct in its use of *be*—both from the habitual *be* in the African American community and from its near-extinct use among European Americans. The shaping of *be(s)* in Lumbee English once again reveals how a dialect community can be resourceful in utilizing present and past linguistic resources to mold and maintain cultural uniqueness through changing social and linguistic circumstances.

The table shows how Lumbee English compares with other dialects with reference to some grammatical patterns.

Cross-Dialectal Comparison of Sentence Structure

Grammatical Structure	Lumbee English	Robeson Eur.-Am. English	Robeson Af.-Am. English	Appal. English	Outer Banks English
finite *bes* e.g. *She bes there*	✓		(✓)		
I'm for *I've* e.g. *I'm been there*	✓				
be for *have* e.g. *they might be lost some inches*	✓				
weren't regularization e.g. *She weren't here*	✓				✓
a-prefixing e.g. *He was a-fishin*	✓			✓	✓
absence of *be* e.g. *They nice, She nice*	(✓)	✓			
verbal *-s* with plural subject e.g. *The dogs get upset*	✓	✓		✓	✓
plural absence with measurement nouns e.g. *twenty mile_*	✓	✓	✓	✓	✓
for to complement e.g. *I want for to get it*	✓			✓	(✓)
completive *done* e.g. *She done messed up*	✓	✓	✓	✓	✓
different irregular forms e.g. *Yesterday she run home; She knowed him*	✓	✓	✓	✓	✓
double modals e.g. *he might could come*	✓	✓	✓	✓	✓

Musician and songwriter Willie French Lowery wrote the music for the outdoor drama, Strike at the Wind.

Like the comparison of vocabulary and pronunciation, the familiar pattern of similarity and difference with other dialects is revealed. Although we do not want to interpret too much into the parallels that emerge between Outer Banks English and Lumbee English, we also cannot deny the fact that they exist, and that some of these similarities unite these dialects in ways that set them apart from other dialects of American English—though Lumbee English and Outer Banks speech remain quite distinct. We must also keep in mind that Lumbee English shares a number of features with highland Southern speech to the west. Such similarities speak to the impact of geographical and cultural separation in the development and maintenance of Lumbee English.

This brief overview of the basic levels of language shows that, for the most part, Lumbee English is not distinguished by structures that are uniquely associated with the Lumbee. Instead, it is the combination of features that makes Lumbee English distinctive. The fact that this variety of English is defined more by its assemblage of dialect forms than by particular, exclusively Lumbee English dialect structures is of little concern to linguists since this is, in fact, how languages usually configure distinct dialects. An extensive survey of American English dialects (Wolfram and

The Dialect Context of Lumbee English

74

Photograph by Neal Hutcheson

Schilling-Estes 1998) shows that this pattern of dialect demarcation is the general and expected way in which virtually all dialects of English are defined.

6

DIALECT AND CULTURE

Photograph by David Oxendine

Photograph by David Oxendine

Objective language facts and the subjective reactions of listeners lead to an unmistakable conclusion: Lumbee English is a distinct, cultural variety of English associated with the Lumbee community in Robeson County. This does not mean that all Lumbee speakers can be identified on the basis of speech any more than we can assume that all Southerners speak Southern English or that all African Americans speak an identifiable African American Vernacular English. There is great speech variation within the community, and individual speakers run the gamut on the dialect scale—from speakers using a fundamental vernacular variety of Lumbee English to those using English that is indistinguishable from mainstream, generic standard English. That is the reality of language and dialect variation. But this truth also cannot deny the conclusion that there has been, and continues to be, a distinctive variety of English associated with the Lumbee speech community.

The current and past linguistic circumstances of the Lumbee certainly underscore their cultural uniqueness on a local level and beyond, demonstrating how their language contributes to their

Traditional Native American dress at pow-wows asserts Indian identity, but the everyday use of dialect is one of the strongest indications of the natural connection between culture and language.

Josh Cummings fishes from the pier at the Indian Cultural Center.

ethnic distinctiveness. Despite persistent institutional efforts to repress and obliterate any linguistic traces of cultural distinctiveness in language and dialect, there remains a strong, symbolic association between language variation and cultural identity. One of the strongest indications of this natural connection between culture and language is found in the fact that language operates on such an unconscious level in its reflection of cultural differences. The Lumbee community did not meet collectively at some point and decide to use certain forms of English in order to demonstrate that they were distinct from other cultural groups. This is not how language differences are implemented; instead, language simply follows the lead of behavioral differences. If there are important cultural differences, language, the most natural behavioral artifact of culture, will unconsciously follow suit. Lumbee English just naturally evolved as the Lumbee community developed.

The facts of Lumbee English demonstrate how community members define themselves and are defined by others through their language. It may not be the language that mainstream government, education, or politics would prefer, but that is irrelevant to the essential cultural association with the community it represents. Study of Lumbee English indicates that it is a robust, distinctive dialect that embodies important dimensions of a community-based culture. That the emblematic role of language has shifted from an ancestral Native American language to a distinctive dialect of English is a testament to the linguistic adaptability, resiliency, and vitality of the Lumbee language community.

APPENDIX

Books, Articles, Theses, and Dissertations on Lumbee English

Atkinson, Tarra Grey. 1995. *The Assessment of Lumbee Vernacular English Speakers: A Sociolinguistic Profile and Application*. MA thesis. Durham, NC: North Carolina Central University.

Barton, Lew. n.d. *Common Lumbee Terms*. Pembroke, NC: Indian Education Resource Center.

Brewer, Jeutonne P. and Robert W. Reising. 1982. Tokens in the pocosin: Lumbee English in North Carolina. *American Speech* 57:108-120.

Dannenberg, Clare J. 1996. *Moving Toward a Diachronic and Synchronic Definition of Lumbee English*. MA thesis. Raleigh, NC: North Carolina State University

Dannenberg, Clare J. 1999. *Sociolinguistic Constructs of Ethnic Identity: The Syntactic Delineation of Lumbee English*. PhD dissertation. Chapel Hill, NC: University of North Carolina at Chapel Hill.

Dannenberg, Clare J. 1999. Grammatical and phonological manifestations of null copula in a tri-ethnic contact situation. *Journal of English Linguistics* 27:356-370.

Dannenberg, Clare J., and Walt Wolfram. 1998. Ethnic identity and grammatical restructuring: *Be(s)* in Lumbee English. *American Speech* 73:139-159.

Dannenberg, Clare J., and Walt Wolfram. 1999. *The Roots of Lumbee English*. Raleigh, NC: North Carolina Language and Life Project.

Dannenberg, Clare J. 2002. *Sociolinguistic Constructs of Ethnic Identity: The Syntactic Delineation of a Native American English Variety*. Publications of the American Dialect Society 87. Durham, NC: Duke University Press.

Hammonds, Renee. 2000. *People's Perceptions of Lumbee Vernacular English*. MA thesis. Durham, NC: North Carolina Central University

Hatch, Leah Joy. 1998. *An Analysis of Irregular Verb Usage in Lumbee English*. MA thesis. Durham, NC: North Carolina Central University.

Herman, David. 2000. Pragmatic constraints on narrative processing: Actants and resolution in a corpus of North Carolina ghost stories. *Journal of Pragmatics* 32:959-1001.

Jackson, Stacie J. 1997. *A Comparative Profile of Vernacular Phonology: Lumbee Vernacular English and African American Vernacular English in Robeson County*. MA thesis. Durham, NC: North Carolina Central University.

Kerns, Ursulla H. 2001. *A Comparison of Lexical Items in Lumbee Vernacular English from the Pembroke and Prospect Communities*. MA thesis. Durham, NC: North Carolina Central University.

Locklear, Hayes Alan, Walt Wolfram, Natalie Schilling-Estes, and Clare Dannenberg. 1999. *Dialect Dictionary of Lumbee English*. Raleigh, NC: North Carolina Language and Life Project.

Miller, Jason Paul. 1996. *Mixed Sociolinguistic Alignment and Ethnic Identity: R-Lessness in a Native American Community*. MA thesis. Raleigh, NC: North Carolina State University.

Schilling-Estes, Natalie. 2000. Investigating intra-ethnic differentiation: /ay/ in Lumbee Native American English. *Language Variation and Change* 12:11-174.

APPENDIX

Torbert, Benjamin. 2000. *Native American Language History Traced through Consonant Cluster Reduction: The Case of Lumbee English*. MA thesis. Raleigh, NC: North Carolina State University.

Torbert, Benjamin. 2001. Language history traced through consonant cluster reduction: The case of Native American Lumbee English. *American Speech* 75:361-387.

Wolfram, Walt. 1996. Delineation and description in dialectology: The case of perfective *I'm* in Lumbee English. *American Speech* 70:5-26.

Wolfram, Walt. 2001. From the brickhouse to the swamp. *American Language Review* 5(4, July/August):34-38.

Wolfram, Walt, and Jason Sellers. 1999. Ethnolinguistic marking of past *be* in Lumbee Vernacular English. *Journal of English Linguistics* 27:94-114.

Wolfram, Walt, and Clare Dannenberg. 1999. Dialect identity in a tri-ethnic context: The case of Lumbee American Indian English. *English World-Wide* 20:179-216.

APPENDIX

REFERENCES

Atkinson, Tarra Grey. 1995. *The Assessment of Lumbee Vernacular English Speakers: A Sociolinguistic Profile and Application.* MA thesis. Durham, NC: North Carolina Central University.

Barton, Lew. n.d. *Common Lumbee Terms.* Pembroke, NC: Indian Education Resource Center.

Brewer, Jeutonne P. and Robert W. Reising. 1982. Tokens in the pocosin: Lumbee English in North Carolina. *American Speech* 57:108-120.

Cassidy, Frederic C. (ed.) 1986, 1991, 1996. *Dictionary of American Regional English.* Cambridge, MA: Harvard/Belknap.

Christian, Donna, Walt Wolfram, and Nanjo Dube. 1989. *Variation and Change in Geographically Isolated Communities: Appalachian and Ozark English.* Publication of the American Dialect Society, No. 74. Tuscaloosa, AL: University of Alabama Press.

Dannenberg, Clare. 1997. Towards the understanding of ethnic distinction and *r*-lessness in multi-ethnic Southern communities: A study of Lumbee Indian Vernacular English. Paper presented at SECOL 58. Lafayette, LA. March, 1998.

Dannenberg, Clare J. 2000. Grammatical and phonological manifestation of null copula in a tri-ethnic contact situation. *Journal of English Linguistics* 27:356-370.

Dannenberg, Clare J. and Walt Wolfram. 1998. Ethnic identity and grammatical restructuring: *Be(s)* in Lumbee English. *American Speech* 73:153-59.

Dial, Adolph. 1993. *The Lumbee*. New York, NY: Chelsea Ridge.

Dial, Adolph, and David K. Eliades. 1975. *The Only Land I Know: A History of the Lumbee Indians*. San Francisco, CA: Indian Historical Press.

Eighty-fourth Congress, Second Session, Public Law 84-570. 1956. *An Act Relating to the Lumbee Indians of North Carolina.*

Evans, William McKee. 1971. *To Die Game: The Story of the Lowry Band, Indian Guerillas of Reconstruction.* Baton Rouge: Louisiana State Press.

Farris, James J. 1925. The Lowrie gang. *Trinity College Historical Society Historical Papers* 15:55-93.

Fernández-Shaw, Carlos M. 1991. *Hispanic Presence in North America from 1492 to Today.* New York: Facts on File.

Fiedel, Stuart J. 1991. Correlating archeology and linguistics: The Algonquian case. *Man in the Northeast* 41:9-32.

Fitch, Edward. 1913. *The First Founders in America, With Facts to Prove That Sir Raleigh's Lost Colony Was Not Lost.* New York: The Society.

Gallatin, Albert. 1836. A synopsis of the Indian Tribes within the United States, east of the Rocky Mountains, and in the British and Russian possessions in North America. *Transactions and Collections of the American Antiquarian Society* 2:1-422.

Gatschet, Albert S. 1900. Grammatic sketch of the Catawba Language. *American Anthropologist* 2:527-549.

Geary, James A., Rev. 1967. The language of the Algonkin tribes. In David B. Quinn (ed.), *The Roanoke voyages, 1584-90*. Works issued by the Haklyut Society, 2nd Series, no. 104. Kraus Reprint 873-900.

Goddard, Ives, ed. 1996. *Handbook of North American Indians.* Washington, D.C.: Smithsonian Institution.

Hakluyt, Richard. 1973. *Virginia Voyages from Haklyut.* Edited by David B. Quinn. Cambridge: Oxford UP.

Hale, Horatio. 1883. The Tutelo tribe and language. *American Philosophical Society* 21:1-47.

Hammonds, Renee. 2000. *People's Perceptions of Lumbee Vernacular English.* MA thesis. Durham, NC: North Carolina Central University

Hariot, Thomas. 1971. [imprinted at London 1588] *Briefe and True Report of the New Found Land in Virginia.* New York. Cap Press

Hazen, Kirk. 1998. The birth of a variant: Evidence for a tripartite negative past *Be* paradigm *Language Variation and Change* 10:221-243.

Hinton, Leanne. 1994. *Flutes of Fire: Essays on California Indian Languages.* Berkeley, CA: Heyday.

Jackson, Stacie J. 1997. *A Comparative Profile of Vernacular Phonology: Lumbee Vernacular English and African American Vernacular English in Robeson County.* MA thesis. Durham, NC: North Carolina Central University.

Kallen, Jeffrey L. 1989. Tense and aspect categories in Irish English. *English World-Wide* 10:1-39.

Kay, Marvin L., and Lorin Lee Cary. 1995. *Slavery in North Carolina, 1748-1775.* University of North Carolina Press. Chapel Hill/London.

Kerns, Ursulla H. 2001. *A Comparison of Lexical Items in Lumbee Vernacular English from the Pembroke and Prospect Communities.* MA thesis. Durham, NC: North Carolina Central University.

Knick, Stanley. 1988. *Robeson Trails Archaeological Survey: Reconnaissance in Robeson County.* Pembroke, NC: Pembroke State University Printing Office.

Knick, Stanley. 1993. *Robeson Crossroads Archaeological Survey: Phase II Testing in Robeson County*. Pembroke, NC: Pembroke State University Printing Office.

Knick, Stanley. 2000. *The Lumbee in Context: Toward an Understanding*. Pembroke, NC: University of North Carolina at Pembroke Printing Office.

Kretzschmar, William A., Virginia G. McDavid, Theodore K. Lerud, and Ellen Johnson. 1994. *Handbook of the Linguistic Atlas of the Middle and South Atlantic States*. Chicago/London: The University of Chicago Press.

Lawson, John. 1952. *Lawson's History of North Carolina*. Edited by Francis Latham Harris. Richmond: Garrett & Massie.

Leap, William L. 1993. *American Indian English*. Salt Lake City, UT: University of Utah Press.

Linguistic Society of America. 1998. Statement on the Ebonics Controversy. Washington, DC: Linguistic Society of America.

Lippi-Green, Rosina. 1997. *English with an Accent: Language Ideology and Discrimination in the United States*. London/New York: Routledge.

Locklear, Hayes Alan, Walt Wolfram, Natalie Schilling-Estes, and Clare Dannenberg. 1999. *A Dialect Dictionary of Lumbee English*. Raleigh, NC: North Carolina Language and Life Project.

Luckenbach, Alvin H., Wayne E. Clark, and Richard S. Levy. 1987. Rethinking cultural stability in Eastern North America prehistory: Linguistic evidence from Eastern Algonquian. *Journal of Middle Atlantic Archeology* 3: 1-33.

Mathis, Mark and Paul Gardner. 1986. Archaeological Survey of the Proposed North Carolina Indian Cultural Center, Robeson County, North Carolina. Raleigh, NC: Office of State Archeology.

REFERENCES

McMillan, Hamilton. 1888. *Sir Walter's Lost Colony*. Raleigh, NC: Edwards and Broughton.

Meyer, Duane. 1961. *The Highland Scots of North Carolina: 1732-1776*. Chapel Hill, NC: University of North Carolina Press.

Miller, Jason P. 1996. *Mixed Sociolinguistic Alignment and Ethnic Identity: R-Lessness in a Native American Community*. MA Thesis. Raleigh, NC: North Carolina State University.

Miller, Lee. 2000. *Roanoke: Solving the Mystery of the Lost Colony*. New York, NY: Arcade.

Montgomery, Michael. 1989. Exploring the roots of Appalachian English. *English World-Wide* 10:227-278.

Montgomery, Michael, and Margaret Mishoe. 1999. "He bes took up with a Yankee girl and moved up there to New York": The verb *Bes* in the Carolinas and its history. *American Speech* 74:240-281.

Montgomery, Michael, and Joseph Hall. forthcoming. *A Dictionary of Smoky Mountain English*. Knoxville, TN: University of Tennessee Press.

Rickford, John R. 1999. *African American Vernacular English: Features, Evolution and Educational Implications*. Malden/Cambridge: Blackwell.

Rudes, Blair A. 1999. *Tuscarora-English/English-Tuscarora Dictionary*. Toronto: University of Toronto Press.

Rudes, Blair. 2001. Resurrecting Coastal Catawban: The reconstructed phonology and morphology of the Woccon language. *Journal of Southern Linguistics* 24:228-244.

Rudes, Blair A. forthcoming. Cofitachique and Yupaha: The ethnicity of a chiefdom. *Anthropological Linguistics*

Rydén, M. and S. Brorström. 1987. *The Be/Have Variation with Intransitives in English*. Stockholm: Almqvist & Wiksell International.

Sabban, Annette. 1984. Investigations into the syntax of Hebridean English. *Scottish Language* 3:5-32.

Schilling-Estes, Natalie. 1998. Situated ethnicities: Constructing and reconstructing identity in the sociolinguistic interview. New Ways of Analyzing Variation 27. Athens, GA. October, 1998.

Schilling-Estes, Natalie. 2000. Investigating intra-ethnic differentiation: /ay/ in Lumbee Native American English. *Language Variation and Change* 12:141-174.

Schilling-Estes, Natalie and Walt Wolfram. 1994. Convergent explanation and alternative regularization: *Were/Weren't* leveling in a vernacular English variety. *Language Variation and Change* 6:273-302.

Schreier, Daniel. 2001. *Nonstandard Grammar and Geographical Isolation: The Genesis and Development of Tristan da Cunha English.* PhD dissertation. Fribourg, Switzerland: University of Fribourg.

Schreier, Daniel. 2002. Terra incognita in the Anglophone world: Tristan da Cunha, South Atlantic Ocean. *English World-Wide* 23:1

Sider, Gerald. M. 1974. *The Political History of the Lumbee Indians of Robeson County, North Carolina.* New School for Social Research thesis.

Siebert, Frank. 1945. Linguistic classification of Catawba. *IJAL* 11:100-4, 211-8.

Silverstein, Michael. 1996. Dynamics of language contact. In Ives Goddard (ed.), *Handbook of North American Languages.* Washington, D.C.: Smithsonian Institution, 117-137

South, Stanley. 1972. *Indians of North Carolina.* Raleigh, NC: State Dept. of Archives and History.

Swanton, John R. 1936. Early history of the Eastern Siouan Tribes. In Robert H. Lowe (ed.), *Essays Presented to A.L Kroeber.* Berkeley, CA: University of California Press, 371-381.

Tagliamonte, Sali A. 1997. Obsolescence in the English perfect? Evidence from Samaná English. *American Speech* 72:33-68.

Thomas, Erik. R. 2001. *An Acoustic Analysis of Vowel Variation in New World English.* Publication of the American Dialects Society 85. Durham, NC: Duke University Press.

Torbert, Benjamin. 2001. Tracing Native American language history through consonant cluster reduction: The case of Lumbee English. *American Speech* 76:361-387.

U.S. Bureau of the Census. *U.S. Census of Population.* 2000. Washington, D.C.: Government Printing Office.

Ward, Trawick. H. 1944. *Indian Communities on the North Carolina Piedmont, AD 1000 to 1700.* Monograph No. 2. Chapel Hill, NC: Research Laboratories of Anthropology.

Weeks, Stephen. 1891. The lost colony of Roanoke: Its fate and survival. *Papers of the American Historical Association* 5(4):107-146.

Wetmore, Ruth Y. 1975. *First on the Land: The North Carolina Indians.* Winston-Salem, NC: J.F. Blair.

Wolfram, Walt. 1980. Dynamic dimensions of language influence: The case of American Indian English. In Howard A. Giles, W. Peter Robinson, and Philip M. Smith (eds.), *Language: Social Psychological Perspectives.* Oxford/New York: Pergammon Press, 377-388.

Wolfram, Walt. 1996. Delineation and description in dialectology: The case of perfective *I'm* in Lumbee English. *American Speech* 71:5-26.

Wolfram, Walt. 2000. On constructing vernacular dialect norms. In Arika Okrent and John Boyle (eds.), *Chicago Linguistic Society 36, The Panels.* Chicago, IL: University of Chicago, 335-358.

Wolfram, Walt, and Donna Christian. 1976. *Appalachian Speech.* Arlington, VA: Center for Applied Linguistics.

Wolfram, Walt, Kirk Hazen, and Natalie Schilling-Estes. 1999. *Dialect Maintenance and Change on the Outer Banks*. Publications of the American Dialect Society 81. Tuscaloosa, AL: University of Alabama Press.

Wolfram, Walt and Natalie Schilling-Estes. 1997. *Hoi Toide on the Outer Banks: The Story of the Ocracoke Brogue*. Chapel Hill, NC: University of North Carolina Press.

Wolfram, Walt and Natalie Schilling-Estes. 1998. *American English: Dialects and Variation*. Malden/Cambridge: Basil Blackwell.

Wolfram, Walt and Jason Sellers. 1999. Ethnolinguistic marking of past *be* in Lumbee Vernacular English. *Journal of English Linguistics* 27:94-114.

Wolfram, Walt, Becky Childs, and Benjamin Torbert. 2000. Tracing language history through consonant cluster reduction: Evidence from isolated dialects. *Southern Journal of Linguistics* 24:17-40.

REFERENCES

REFERENCES

93

Printed in the USA
CPSIA information can be obtained
at www.ICGtesting.com
CBHW041921031123
1680CB00013B/192